SHE DID IT!

21 WOMEN

WHO CHANGED THE WAY WE THINK

acknowledgments

Work on this book began with Jodi Lipson at AARP. My involvement is due to my agent,
Susan Cohen. Thanks to them, I have learned a great deal about remarkable women.
Jodi, along with Cindy Kane, read all the lives with impressive care. Thank you to our authenticity
readers, to Karen O. Kupperman, as well as to the Mohegan tribe, for their insightful feedback.
I am grateful to Rotem Moscovich, her able assistant Heather Crowley,
and uncannily skillful copy editors David Jaffe and Guy Cunningham,
who were all committed to excellence.
Finally, the design was expertly overseen by Joann Hill.
Thank you, everyone, for a remarkable team effort.

Library of Congress Cataloging-in-Publication Data
Names: McCully, Emily Arnold, author.
Title: She did it! : 21 women who changed the way we think / by Emily Arnold McCully.
Description: First edition. • Los Angeles ; New York : Disney/Hyperion, [2018]
Identifiers: LCCN 2018014928 • ISBN 9781368019910 (hardcover)
ISBN 1368019919 (hardcover)
Subjects: LCSH: Women—Biography—Juvenile literature.
Women—History—Juvenile literature. • Feminism—History—Juvenile literature.
Classification: LCC HQ1123.M395 2018 • DDC 920.72—dc23
LC record available at https://lccn.loc.gov/2018014928
Reinforced binding
Visit www.DisneyBooks.com

SHE DID IT!

21 WOMEN

WHO CHANGED THE WAY WE THINK

CALDECOTT MEDAL WINNER

Emily Arnold McCully

Disney • HYPERION

Los Angeles   New York

to every girl who
intends to help make the
world a better one

table of contents

IDA MINERVA TARBELL

pioneer investigative journalist

1857–1944

Ida Minerva Tarbell pioneered investigative journalism. At a time when the press would print anything that sold papers or magazines, Tarbell had a passion for facts. With a talent for finding buried secrets and the people willing to share them, Ida took on one of the most powerful men in the United States: John D. Rockefeller. The articles she wrote about his Standard Oil Company showed that it had succeeded by using unfair and illegal methods—and led to new laws about what businesses can and can't do. Ida Tarbell's career reminds us that a democracy must have fearless and accurate reporting for the people to be served.

ida tarbell was born on November 5, 1857, on her grandmother's little farm in western Pennsylvania. Two years later, the Drake well struck petroleum (oil) just a few miles away. For the first time, people had figured out how to extract it from the ground. Oil was an ideal fuel to light lamps, grease machine parts to work smoothly, and, later, to run automobiles.

Thousands of people hoping to get rich quick rushed to western Pennsylvania to dig their own wells. Ida's father, Franklin Tarbell, went there, too. Ida's new home was surrounded by tree stumps, filthy oil spills, ghastly oil fires, horses that got stuck in the mud and died, bad smells, and deafening noises.

a curious child

Ida was a bright little girl, tall for her age, with a curiosity that got her in trouble at times. Once she tossed her baby brother into a creek to see if he would float. (He did.) Another time, she sneaked into a room to peer at the body of a woman who had burned up in a stove fire. That adventure brought on endless nightmares.

Ida read the Bible, but she was more interested in science. People who figured the Earth's age based on what the Bible said believed it was six thousand years old, but the scientists Ida read said the Earth was much older. This was a shocking denial of Biblical teaching. So, too, was Charles Darwin's book *On the Origin of Species*, published in 1859, which said animals and humans had a common ancestor: the ape. Ida was desperate for the truth. She wrestled with the differences between science and the Bible, and, on the topic of evolution, chose to believe science. It wasn't an easy decision to make. No one in the family agreed with her.

After truth, Ida's second great passion was fairness, and that is why John D. Rockefeller made her angry. Rockefeller owned a company called Standard Oil which used underhanded methods to drive small oil producers like Ida's father out of business. The unfairness of Rockefeller's practices and his contempt for the truth disgusted Ida.

rockefeller and standard oil

John D. Rockefeller, born in 1839, showed a precocious gift for making money. By age twenty, he had formed his own wholesale grocery company in Cleveland, Ohio. When the Drake well succeeded, he saw a new opportunity: refining, or turning raw petroleum into the kerosene that lit lamps around America.

Starting in 1863, Rockefeller bought one refinery, then built another. He branched out, buying land to make barrels, warehouses, and boats to store and transport oil. In time, his company, Standard Oil, controlled nearly all the oil refineries and pipelines in the United States. But Standard didn't make its money honestly. Rockefeller crushed his competition by making secret deals with the railroads that carried oil to his refineries. He cut prices to force other companies out of business, then bought them up. After investigations like Tarbell's turned the public against him, he gave away millions of dollars, becoming one of America's most important philanthropists.

Fairness was an issue for Ida at home, too. Her father controlled the family finances, leaving her mother feeling powerless. Marriage itself seemed unfair. Ida began to realize that a career in any field would be difficult, if not impossible, if she were required to serve and obey a husband. She wanted to support herself and control her own life. When she was fourteen, she vowed never to marry.

women's education

Ida was a serious girl and believed her life must have a purpose. By the time she graduated from high school, she had decided to become a biologist. That meant going to college. But few colleges admitted women. Nearby Allegheny College was one that did.

Ida was the only girl in her freshman class at Allegheny. At the time, it was widely believed that academic study—especially in the sciences—was harmful to women's brains and reproductive organs. Ida was aware that her male classmates thought that having a woman in their classes meant the material had to be simplified. She was shy to begin with, and their disapproval made her acutely uncomfortable. It wasn't long before she and the handful of intelligent girls who joined her won them over. And the lessons were not simplified.

Ida was lucky to find a sympathetic science professor who encouraged her to be a biologist. The scientific methods she learned—look beneath the surface, find proof—would later help make her a superb reporter.

becoming a journalist

Ida had only two choices as a woman college graduate: teach or become a missionary in her parents' Methodist church. She took a job teaching at a school in Ohio. After two years of being overworked and underpaid, she returned to her family home in Pennsylvania, where her microscope was waiting. She hoped she could do some independent research. But very quickly the Reverend Theodore Flood came to dinner and asked her to help out on the magazine he edited, the *Chautauquan*. She accepted.

The *Chautauquan* was published by the Chautauqua movement. This group offered lectures and seminars by renowned figures on its campus in western New York and mail-order courses for people at home. Ida's broad education and intense curiosity made her the ideal person to answer questions from readers who had no reference books at home and were confused by articles in the magazine.

She was a natural at journalism and enjoyed working with the magazine's employees. They were mostly women and became Ida's friends. She mastered all the details of magazine production and became indispensable to the editor. When her first articles were published, she was thrilled to see her name in print.

Ida stayed with the magazine for six years. In that time, the steel, oil, and railroad businesses grew quickly. Wealth in these industries was concentrated among a small number of "robber barons," men who grew rich at a time when government did not regulate businesses. Immigrant labor was cheap, and natural resources and the environment were not protected. Ida personally kept up with national and world events—and she thought the *Chautauquan* should pay more attention to them, too. "All about me were people who at least believed themselves materially secure," she said. "They lived comfortably within their means, they were busy keeping things as they were, preserving what they had." Ida didn't want to be comfortable—she wanted to be challenged and take part in the world. She was almost thirty and wondered: Did she have a future at the *Chautauquan?* What, now, was the purpose of her life?

To find out, she took a bold step. In 1890, she quit her job and moved to Paris. She had one hundred dollars in her pocket and no job prospects, except the slim hope she could sell articles about France to US newspapers.

breaking free

Paris in 1890 was in its Belle Époque, a time between wars when many French people were well off and enjoyed the arts. But Ida lived hand to mouth. Once she even pawned her coat. Still, the city thrilled her, and she managed, in time, to sell articles. She made friends and visited salons—intellectual discussion groups—led by women. She dreamed of having her own salon.

Tarbell was planning to make Paris her permanent home. Then one day, a sandy-haired, blue-eyed, fast-talking Irish American bounded up four flights to her rented room. He introduced himself as Sam McClure and asked her to join his brand-new magazine in New York. Ida had heard of him. McClure was a brilliant, ambitious man, blessed with charm. Alas, there was no money to fund the flood of ideas he had for his magazine—though he didn't tell Ida that. (She soon found out.)

Ida Tarbell stayed in Paris, sending articles to *McClure's*. But Sam kept begging until she came back to the United States to join the staff. Before long, she and her colleagues would include all the great "muckrakers." They were a new kind of reporter: one who investigated corruption that hurt ordinary people.

pioneer muckraker

At first, the new magazine struggled to find subscribers who would pay to receive it every month. McClure, on a hunch, decided that a series of articles about Napoleon Bonaparte, who had once ruled as emperor of France, would attract readers. It did. *McClure's* circulation doubled.

Next, McClure assigned Tarbell to write about an American hero, Abraham Lincoln. She was to roam the nation, interviewing people who had known the president. A lone woman on the road made people suspicious at first, but she won their trust and gathered a load of stories.

Tarbell already worshipped Lincoln. To her, he had had the same disappearing pioneer values as her father: He was smart, skilled, brave, honest, and witty. Her twelve-part Lincoln series ran in 1895–96 and boosted the magazine's circulation again, to over three hundred thousand, higher than that of any rival magazine.

In 1899, McClure brought Tarbell back to New York to be the magazine's desk editor (manager). McClure was in and out of the office, always in a state of nervous excitement, full of ideas, ordering his staff to go out and find more news! He needed a cool head to keep order, and Ida Tarbell had one. She quickly earned the respect and affection of her colleagues.

McClure's had exposed corruption in city governments and on Wall Street, New York City's financial center. President Teddy Roosevelt, who favored new laws to protect the people from dishonest business, took notice. But sending reporters around the country to write great stories was expensive, and *McClure's* finances were shaky. Tarbell and her editors needed to find another great story.

Sam McClure's idea was *trusts*, a secretive method of organizing businesses to help them defeat the competition. Several trusts had recently been formed in the steel, sugar, coal, and oil industries. But what was the hook that would grab the world's attention? One day as Tarbell began musing about her childhood in the oil regions, her colleagues realized their subject was John D. Rockefeller's Standard Oil Company—and Tarbell was the one to write about it.

the history of standard oil

Word of the new project got out. People warned Tarbell that the secretive and vindictive Rockefeller would ruin the magazine. With so much at stake for the powerful company—nicknamed "the Octopus" for the many businesses and politicians it controlled—she herself might be harmed. Sources in the oil business would refuse to give her information about Standard. Ida ignored the threats.

Congress had investigated Standard Oil's practices several times, so Tarbell assumed she would simply read through all the records. But she soon discovered that most of the crucial records had been hidden or destroyed. Tarbell kept digging and even interviewed Standard employees when she could. One executive at Standard, Henry Rogers, actually offered to speak to her, thinking she'd write flattering things about him. He put a stop to their meetings when she learned too much from other sources. However badly Standard Oil had treated her father, Ida wrote a fair history of the company and its rapid rise to power over the oil industry.

Tarbell's series about Standard Oil began in *McClure's* in 1902 and ran for nineteen installments. It proved the company had gotten discounted rates for shipping oil through dishonest practices, giving Standard an edge over the competition to smash it out completely. Facts were what mattered to Tarbell. Her case was airtight. Tarbell's exposé of Standard Oil was as popular and interesting as a thriller.

More important, her articles changed public opinion and got the government to act. In 1911, the US Supreme Court ruled that Standard Oil had broken the law. The giant company was forced to divide into smaller pieces.

Ida Tarbell was forty-eight when the series was completed. In 1904, her book *The History of the Standard Oil Company* was published, becoming the most important business book of the century.

democracy dies in darkness

Even when Tarbell was well into her eighties, the press continued to ask her opinions on important questions of the day. She always responded modestly and clearly. Her celebrity faded a little but never disappeared. She had fought tirelessly for fairness, ethics, and a United States of America where everyone could make a living. She had helped to invent investigative journalism. In today's era of fake news and "curated news," where people can read only what they want to, the United States needs honest, thorough reporting more than ever for democracy to survive.

muckrakers

In 1906, President Theodore Roosevelt coined the term *muckraker* to describe journalists who were seeking to expose scandals and corruption among political and business leaders. "The men with the muck rakes are often indispensable to the well-being of society," he remarked in a speech. But he also thought journalists were going too far in their exposés, accusing them of concentrating only on the negative, like the man with the muck rake in John Bunyan's *Pilgrim's Progress*. As an exasperated Tarbell pointed out, the man in Bunyan's tale was a symbol of the corrupt rich who could not take their eyes off their dirty muck—not of those exposing them. Still, the term muckraker stuck.

"The quest of the truth had been born in me—
the most tragic and incomplete, as well as
the most essential, of man's quests."

—ida tarbell

JANE
ADDAMS

champion of immigrants and the poor

1860–1935

As tenements in US cities filled with immigrants in the late 1800s, Jane Addams changed the way people thought about the poor. Before then, Americans mostly depended on relatives and religious organizations for help during hard times. But when waves of immigrants arrived, often without family, their needs overwhelmed private charities. In 1889, Addams founded Hull House in Chicago's factory district to try to improve the lives of its residents. On a wider scale, Addams became a potent political force—a leader in the battle against child labor and for education, a crusader for women's suffrage and world peace. In 1931, she was awarded the Nobel Peace Prize.

jane addams was born on September 6, 1860, in Cedarville, Illinois,

the eighth of nine children. Her father, John Addams, was a well-to-do mill owner and banker. A state senator and strong supporter of Abraham Lincoln, he helped found the Illinois Republican Party. Partly because she associated Lincoln with her father, Jane credited the president with influencing her life and work. John Addams, like "Honest Abe," was known for his integrity. Even during the Civil War, when contracts to supply the Union Army went to businesses with political connections, no one ever dared try to bribe John Addams for favors. Jane adored her high-minded father. But she constantly worried that she was falling short of his expectations.

a childhood of loss

Jane Addams lost her mother when she was two. At four, she contracted tuberculosis of the spine. She saw herself as an "ugly pigeon-toed little girl, whose crooked back obliged her to walk with her head held . . . upon one side." Her appearance made her painfully self-conscious but also deeply sympathetic to others.

One day, she went with her father to a nearby mill in the poorest section of town. As she later recalled: "On that day I had my first sight of the poverty. . . . I remember launching at my father the pertinent inquiry why people lived in such horrid little houses so close together, and . . . I declared with much firmness when I grew up I should, of course, have a large house, but it would . . . [be built] . . . right in the midst of horrid little houses like these."

She was expressing the prejudice people often feel toward the poor, yet with no inclination to separate herself from them.

A desire to help others was central to Jane's personality. So was a strong sense of responsibility. But when she was young, she lacked the confidence to carry out these feelings, as a dream once illustrated: Everyone else in the world was dead, and it was up to her to reinvent a wagon wheel. There was a forge in the dream, but she could only stare at it, paralyzed, not knowing where to start.

Wanting to care for others, Jane planned to become a doctor, a remarkable idea for a girl at that time. The first woman doctor, Elizabeth Blackwell, had graduated in the mid-1800s, and by 1880, only about twenty-four hundred women practiced medicine in the country. At a time when women were discouraged from every profession, Jane thought studying science would make others take her seriously. But few institutions offered even a bachelor's degree to women. Jane set her sights on one of them, Smith College.

Her father (who remarried when Jane was eight) seems never to have praised or encouraged her. He refused to let her go to Smith, ordering her instead to attend the local Rockford Seminary. He argued that her first duty would always be to her family. Jane was crushed, but she obeyed him.

Rockford turned out to have an excellent faculty. Most important to Jane's future, she found a group of serious-minded classmates who loved to discuss ideas, especially those surrounding the battle for women's rights. Her closest friend was Ellen Gates Starr, who was as cheerful and lively as Jane was passionate and serious.

searching for purpose

Jane graduated at the top of her class and planned to go to Smith to prepare for medical school. Again, her father put his foot down, saying her duty was to family. Soon after, he died suddenly of a ruptured appendix. Jane was devastated. The meaning was ripped from her life. But her father's death also opened a door.

Jane, her sister, and her stepmother decided to move to Philadelphia to join Jane's stepbrother who studied medicine there. Jane enrolled in Philadelphia Women's Medical College.

But worsening pain from her childhood spine ailment soon sent her to the hospital. She lay strapped to a bed for six months. She was told her back was too weak for her to ever have children. She didn't return to college, but she recovered enough to travel.

In Europe she wrestled with herself over how she could carry on her father's greatness. She spent two years visiting cathedrals and museums, even a bullfight, but she was most drawn to the poorer districts of cities. She saw there were ways other than practicing medicine to help the needy. One was the new "settlement movement," in which volunteers lived in a lower-income area and offered education, health care, and other services to poor people. As factory-manufacturing in cities replaced individual skilled work, crowded city slums were increasingly filled with people unable to earn enough to support their families.

Her curiosity about the settlement movement took her to East London's Toynbee Hall, founded in 1884 to try to address increasing poverty. Toynbee Hall provided lodging and a center where wealthy university graduates could live among and help the poor. The goal of its founders was to end poverty altogether. Jane Addams was deeply moved by what she saw.

She decided to found her own settlement house. She talked it over with Ellen Starr, who was now teaching in Chicago. Ellen, whose nature was to see possibilities rather than difficulties, readily agreed to be Jane's partner. Their settlement house would be located in an industrial neighborhood in Chicago where struggling factory workers and immigrant families lived.

attitudes toward poverty before jane addams

Until Jane Addams brought the settlement movement to America, attitudes toward poor people were often negative. If people were strong enough to work, the reasoning went, then it was their own fault if they couldn't support their families. In 1855, an article in the *New York Times* described parts of the city "crowded with the poorest" where "lazy, loafing men" were hanging around. So poor people were sent to dreaded places called poorhouses and forced to work in dirty conditions for bad food. Their children went to orphanages, where conditions weren't much better.

charity begins at home

Addams and Starr developed their mission statement: "To provide a center for a higher civic and social life; to institute and maintain educational and philanthropic enterprises and to investigate and improve the conditions in the industrial districts of Chicago." The term *higher* showed that they believed in promoting culture—art, music, and literature—as a way of uplifting the poor. Theirs was a lofty purpose. In a society that had suddenly produced extremes of wealth and poverty, they wanted everyone to have equal opportunities. They would use trial and error to determine what worked. After years of passivity and doubt, Addams had a clear goal and was bursting with energy and ideas.

The old mansion they leased, Hull House, had been built decades earlier. At times it had contained a shop, a home for the elderly, and a factory. The attic was said to be haunted. The surrounding streets stank of uncollected garbage. The mostly foreign-born residents didn't know how to demand city services, and their elected officials were famously corrupt.

Into that setting, Addams moved with her family heirlooms, paintings, and silver to create an atmosphere of beauty and comfort for her clients. She and Starr began raising money from donors. Their mostly Irish, German, and Polish neighbors greeted the women with suspicion. Why were such well-off single women moving there? Boys threw stones that broke the windows.

an idea takes shape

Addams and Starr opened a day care center, the city's first kindergarten, clubs for boys and girls, handicrafts classes, and a battered-wife shelter. They added a coffeehouse, gymnasium, and swimming pool. Before long, the women were nursing the sick, washing newborns, and preparing corpses for burial. Hull House was becoming the heart of the community.

By its second year, two thousand people were showing up every week, wanting help and advice and using Hull House's programs. Education—always Addams's first priority—was offered at every level, from kindergarten to night school college courses. There were music lessons, a lending library, a drama group, discussion groups of every kind, and an employment office. Helping workers find jobs also meant helping them join unions to bargain for better wages and conditions so they would not be at the mercy of employers. Residents were consulted on each new undertaking, neighborhood girls assisted in children's classes, and young men taught in the gymnasium.

Hull House attracted more young women committed to social work. In addition to running the various programs, these women tried to solve pressing issues of the day. Addams and her associates investigated and protested dangerous working conditions, especially for children, and asked their clients if their families had nutritious meals.

Every day some crisis seemed to arise—and with it a new lesson. On their first Christmas, for example, Hull House handed out candy to the children. Several girls refused it: They worked in a candy factory and couldn't stand the sight of it. After a small boy was killed in an accident at a factory, Addams discovered the owners had made his parents sign a form saying the company was not responsible for "carelessness."

Addams became increasingly political. She pushed the city of Chicago to pass laws to improve safety, health, and sanitation. She pressed for laws to make all children go to school. When the mayor appointed Addams its first female garbage inspector, it was hot news. The publicity helped her to battle corruption and injustice.

onto the world stage

As she played a bigger part in city life, Addams was appointed to Chicago's Board of Education. And when workers at the Pullman Company struck for higher wages, disrupting train travel all over the country, she was the one who stepped in.

the pullman strike of 1894

The Pullman Car Works in southern Chicago built railroad cars—and dominated the lives of its workers. They labored sixteen hours a day, and many lived in poor housing in Pullman's company town. When the company cut its workers' pay by 30 percent, it made no cuts in the cost of rent and said it would fire workers who didn't live in their town. Near starvation, the workers went on strike in May 1894. Other railroad workers joined the strike until two hundred thousand people had stopped working.

It was Addams who tried to listen to all sides of the issue. A reporter who heard her speak to the strikers' leaders said her face was a "window behind which stands her soul." She did not waver. The government finally ended the strike.

Jane Addams and her little army of women in Hull House were a movement for big reforms. Addams refused to accept that there were two Americas, divided into the upper class and lower class. Her speeches and books eloquently spread her message of social justice.

In 1898, the United States declared war on Spain and invaded Cuba and other Spanish colonies. Addams and many others considered the war imperialist—one country trying to take over another—and contrary to US principles of democracy. After the United States won the war and took possession of Cuba, she became a pacifist.

Years later, in an effort to stop World War I before it started, Addams sailed on a "Peace Ship" to a conference of women pacifists in Europe. In the United States, some peace agitators were sent to jail for speaking out against war. Addams remained free, but the Daughters of the American Revolution expelled her, and she was strongly criticized by other groups. Still, she never lessened her efforts. She served as president of the International League for Peace and Freedom for ten years. For that work, she received the Nobel Peace Prize in 1931, the first American woman to win the award.

Despite her back problems, Addams enjoyed good health through decades of demanding activism until 1926, when she suffered a heart attack. She was never very well again and died on May 21, 1935. Her funeral was held in the courtyard at Hull House.

We are a more tolerant, caring nation now than we were during her lifetime. But there is more work to do, and the wise and compassionate voice of Jane Addams is much needed. The problems she tried to solve are again—or perhaps still—with us.

*"The good we secure for ourselves
is precarious and uncertain
until it is secured for all of us
and incorporated into
our common life."*

—jane addams

in an 1892 speech

MADAM C. J. WALKER

millionaire businesswoman and philanthropist

1867–1919

Sarah Breedlove's transformation from a child of slaves to a woman of fabulous wealth is an incredible rags-to-riches tale. That it took place during the time called "Jim Crow" makes her story even more astonishing. The South had lost the Civil War, and former slaves were now free citizens. But they risked violence and even murder if they acted like they were equal to whites. In this era, Breedlove built a hair-care products business that was so successful, she became the first self-made woman millionaire in America. Madam C. J. Walker, as she called herself, used much of her fortune to help other African Americans have better lives.

sarah breedlove was the first person in her family to be born into freedom—just two years after the end of slavery. Her parents were poor sharecroppers on a Louisiana cotton plantation.

sharecropping

After slaves were freed, plantation owners still needed workers, and the freed slaves needed jobs. Sharecropping was in reality a system of forced labor that made it impossible for former slaves to escape poverty—a way to extend slavery by another name. Plantation owners gave former slaves a portion of the land to use in exchange for a share of the crop. By the time they paid for rent, food, seeds, and equipment—bought from the plantation owner—the workers were never able to get ahead. In fact, they often owed the *owners* money. Sharecroppers could not leave the plantation or they would face arrest.

Sarah picked cotton in the fields and never went to school. Black schools were routinely torched by the Ku Klux Klan. Members of this group were white men who used violence to terrorize newly freed slaves.

Sarah's parents both died from yellow fever when she was seven, leaving her an orphan. An older brother moved to Vicksburg, Mississippi, to find work. Sarah and her older sister, Louvenia, had to support themselves by taking in washing from white families. For a dollar a week, they hauled heavy loads of laundry, beat the clothes with wooden sticks against washboards, then scrubbed the cloth with lye soaps that burned their skin. When it seemed their dreary existence could get no worse, yellow fever spread through the neighborhood again in 1878, killing three thousand people. With few people to work in the fields, the cotton crop failed. The Breedlove sisters picked up and left for Vicksburg, too.

backbreaking work

There the sisters resumed their work as washerwomen. Sarah's sister married, probably to find some security. Her husband was cruel to Sarah. To get away from her brother-in-law, Sarah found her own husband, Moses, when she was fourteen. Along the way, she began teaching herself to read. At seventeen, she gave birth to a baby girl. The daughter, Lelia, brought light and purpose into Sarah's life.

When Lelia was two, Moses was killed in an accident. Sarah had to support herself and Lelia. She was determined to grow her business and be the best laundress in Vicksburg. But she began thinking of moving again—this time to St. Louis, Missouri. For the rest of her life she would move often, always looking to rise in the world.

segregated st. louis

Segregation was the law in St. Louis, the third largest city in the country. Segregation was enforced by new "Jim Crow" laws throughout the South. But even a segregated city offered opportunity, if you worked hard, and Sarah heard that laundresses earned more in St. Louis than in Vicksburg. She and Lelia moved there in 1887.

Three of Sarah's four brothers were in town, so Sarah was with family again. Despite having no electricity or running water, she managed to set up a laundry business again and to do odd jobs, including work in a kitchen. She joined St. Paul's, a Black church where she met people of great dignity. Sarah tried to behave as they did.

One day, she worked up the nerve to address the Sunday school. She spoke about an elderly blind man who was desperate for money to support himself and his disabled sister. Her listeners were moved and gave money for the man. It was the first time she showed her gift for helping others. Through the church, Sarah met people who had risen in Black society. She saw that their education helped lift them out of poverty.

unhealthy hair

Sarah kept working on self-improvement, going to night school and saving up to send Lelia to college. She married, for the second time, to a man named John Davis, whom she would later divorce. The laundry business brought in $1.50 a day. Then Sarah noticed something that would start her on a new career. She was losing her hair. Her scalp was always itching and inflamed.

Sarah wasn't the only Black woman with hair loss. A'Lelia Bundles, Sarah's great-great-granddaughter and biographer, explained: "During the early 1900s, when most Americans lacked indoor plumbing and electricity, bathing was a luxury. As a result, Sarah and many other women were going bald because they washed their hair so infrequently." Pollution, bacteria, and lice could all damage unwashed hair. So could hair-care products and methods for straightening hair.

straightening hair: a controversy

After slavery ended, some African American women tried to straighten their coarse, tightly curled hair to meet white standards of beauty in an effort to be accepted by a predominantly white society. One method for straightening hair was to wrap it tightly. A woman twisted and pulled her hair and tied it with strings. Her scalp hurt for days afterward. Products to achieve straight hair were advertised beginning in the 1830s. One mail-order product was a liquid that women applied to freshly washed hair and then ironed with a hot, flat iron. The process caused many women to suffer burns to their scalps.

While the makers of such products claimed that Black women would look more "socially acceptable" with straight hair, many Black women argued that their Afro-textured hair reflected their African ancestry—something of which they were proud. The Black educator and civil rights leader Booker T. Washington and his wife spoke out against hair-straightening. They said Black women should not imitate white standards of beauty.

In slavery, Black women had been punished for trying to improve their appearance. Now that they were free, many cared a great deal about grooming. It brought not just pride in appearance, but opportunity and social standing as well.

Sarah Breedlove hungered for all those things. She was determined to carry herself with as much pride as the Black celebrities who came to the St. Louis

World's Fair in 1904. That seemed impossible unless she could repair her hair.

One day a newspaper ad caught her eye. "The Wonderful Hair Grower" was an herb-and-egg mixture marketed by Annie Turnbo, who claimed it repaired and straightened Black women's hair. At the time, hair products for women were sold door-to-door. In addition to her laundry business, Sarah became a sales agent for Turnbo's product and used it herself.

Around this time, she began dating a slick salesman named C. J. Walker.

the formula

At her washtubs one day, Sarah faced a hard truth: "I said to myself, 'What are you going to do when you grow old and your back gets stiff? Who is going to take care of your little girl?'" The answer was, she would start her own business. She would mix up a hair product and sell it herself. Years later she claimed she'd been given the formula in a dream: "A big black man appeared to me and told me what to mix up for my hair. Some of the remedy was grown in Africa, but I sent for it, put it on my scalp, and in a few weeks my hair was coming in faster than it had ever fallen out."

The ingredients for Madam C. J. Walker's Wonderful Hair Grower included a petroleum base, beeswax, copper sulfate and sulphur for sanitizing and healing, violet extract, and carbolic acid. She later added other products to her offerings, such as a vegetable shampoo. Her products didn't make hair straighter. She said she didn't want to imitate whites. But she did sell an oil called Glossine that protected hair that was being straightened with a hot comb.

Annie Turnbo's company already had the St. Louis market covered, so Breedlove decided to move again. In 1905, she went west to Denver, Colorado. One of her brothers had settled there, and it had never been a slave town. She continued to take in laundry, but only for two days a week. The rest of her week was devoted to mixing her product, demonstrating it around the city, and advertising it. C. J. Walker joined her in Denver, and they married in 1910. Sarah intended to have her husband work for her, not the other way around. He became her business partner.

the invention of madam c. j. walker

In the early 1900s, many women who owned businesses, especially those who sold cosmetics, called themselves "Madam" such-and-such. The word made them sound French, and French women were thought to possess the secrets of beauty. Sarah Breedlove became Madam C. J. Walker.

Her husband supported her, to a point.

"When we began to make ten dollars a day, he thought that was enough, thought I ought to be satisfied," Madam C. J. Walker once said. "But I was convinced that my hair preparation would fill a long-felt want. And when we found it impossible to agree, due to his narrowness of vision, I embarked on business for myself."

She worked hard. Later she would tell how she went house to house, selling her hair products to Black women. "After a while," she said, "I got going pretty well," even though she had many disappointments before she found success.

As part of her grooming business, Walker and her daughter went to Pittsburgh and founded Lelia College for "hair culturists" in 1908. Lelia, who had gone to college for a year, now managed the school, which trained women to sell Walker products. Madam and C. J. Walker moved on to Indianapolis, at the time a great center for commerce. They built a beauty school, factory, and laboratory. Madam Walker had agents selling her products coast to coast now.

The eye-catching ads that Walker placed in Black-owned newspapers kept some of the papers in business. Designed to look like news articles, they featured Madam C. J. Walker's own face and hair as "before and after" examples. Her marketing included a social message: her careful grooming and beauty products encouraged Black women to care for themselves.

Many of her satisfied customers became agents, trained in the Walker System at Walker's beauty schools. Soon, she had thousands of "Walker agents," all proud of how they looked. They had pride in themselves and were willing to step forth in the world. Many started their own businesses.

Madam C. J. Walker divorced her third husband in 1912, although she kept his name. As the now-famous business expanded still more, she continued to educate her sales agents. They were instructed to tell the story of Walker's life to new customers. Every agent had to truly believe in the mission. "Open your own shop," Walker urged them. "Secure prosperity and freedom." The agents who started their own shops were required to use Walker products in them. Today we would call this sort of business a *franchise*. By 1911, Madam Walker was making $3,000 a week. That was more than $70,000 in today's dollars.

she insists on being recognized

In 1912, the National Negro Business League met in Chicago. Walker was determined to address its two hundred delegates. But Booker T. Washington, its founder, controlled the agenda. For two days, Walker tried to catch his eye, and every time he ignored her, even after a newspaper publisher stood and asked Washington to hear what she had to say. He continued to ignore her.

The next day, she waved her hand again. Washington looked away. That was the last straw for Walker. Nearly six feet tall, she rose to her majestic height and announced that she was in a business that benefited her race: "I am a woman who came from the cotton fields of the South. I was promoted from there to the washtub. Then I was promoted to the cook kitchen, and from there I promoted myself into the business of manufacturing hair goods and preparations. I have built my own factory on my own ground. My object in life is not simply to make money for myself or to spend it on myself. I love to use a part of what I make trying to help others." By all accounts, she impressed him.

Madam Walker traveled tirelessly, managing every aspect of her thriving business. She became the first self-made woman millionaire in America, one who made her money herself rather than inheriting it from wealthy parents.

Called the "money-making wonder of the age" by a journalist, she also gave lots of it away. Thousands of dollars went to the founding of the NAACP, and thousands more to combat lynching, the practice of murdering African Americans as a way of terrorizing Black people. She gave generously to churches and YMCAs, as well as cultural centers and scholarships for young people. When the nation was wracked by race riots after World War I, she was a signer of a telegram to President Woodrow Wilson protesting the violence and injustice rampant in America.

the naacp

The NAACP—the National Association for the Advancement of Colored People—was founded by white and Black activists in 1909 to help bring justice to African Americans. The founders were motivated by a race riot the year before in Springfield, Illinois, Lincoln's home town, and a sharp rise in the number of lynchings. The oldest civil rights group in the US, the NAACP joined important court battles to help African Americans achieve equality and published a report on the horrific practice of lynching. In the 1950s, it would help advance the landmark lawsuit that outlawed segregation in public schools.

mother and daughter moguls

In 1913, at the age of nineteen, Lelia opened a beauty parlor in Harlem, a neighborhood in New York City. Walker commissioned a magnificent double town house for it: the Walker Studio and the Dark Tower. It became the place to be during the Harlem Renaissance. Beautiful Lelia, statuesque like her mother, renamed herself A'Lelia and presided over an ongoing party for artists and intellectuals.

the harlem renaissance

The Harlem Renaissance is a name given to a cultural movement located in the New York City neighborhood of Harlem. Beginning in the 1920s, African American writers, musicians, actors, and artists mingled in Harlem and produced exciting contributions to American culture.

People flocked to Harlem's music clubs to hear blues singers like Bessie Smith and bands with legendary leaders such as Duke Ellington and Cab Calloway. Magazine and book publishers produced works of literature by African American writers such as Zora Neale Hurston, W.E.B. Du Bois, Langston Hughes, Jean Toomer, Countee Cullen, and Nella Larsen.

This blossoming of culture by and for African Americans showed that Black artists could be free to create whatever they wanted to. In the words of poet Langston Hughes, "We will stand on top of the mountain, free within ourselves."

In 1916, Madam Walker had a villa built on the Hudson River in nearby Irvington and called it Lewaro (after the first letters of her daughter's name: Lelia Walker Robinson). It was opulently furnished and contained an automated pipe organ that played at the touch of a button, a gold music room, and a vast library of books bound in leather.

But Madam Walker, who moved into the mansion in 1918, had little time to enjoy it. The hard work she had done all her life had taken a toll on her body. She had high blood pressure and probably a bad heart. In 1919, she was rushed to Lewaro in a private railroad car from an appearance in St Louis. Some days later, her nurse heard her say, "I want to live to help my race." They were her last words.

According to one account, she left two-thirds of her money to Black charities, generous to the end.

"Don't sit down and wait for the opportunities to come. Get up and make them."

—madam c. j. walker

ISADORA DUNCAN

founder of modern dance

1877–1927

Isadora Duncan burst onto a dance world ruled by the rigid movements and costumes of classical ballet, and transformed dance forever. Thrilling and shocking audiences in America and Europe, she created an art from natural movement and the beauty of the human body. Today, because of Isadora's influence, hundreds of companies perform modern dance, and much classical ballet now incorporates its greater freedom of expression. Isadora went beyond liberating dance; she freed women from constricting movement and fashions.

San Francisco was still a wild frontier town when **isadora duncan** was born on May 26, 1877, the youngest of four children. After the Gold Rush, California remained a magnet for people hoping to get rich. All kinds came, looking for the excitement of the new. It was the last frontier.

Even by San Francisco standards, the Duncan family was unconventional. Isadora's father, a businessman, called himself the authority on all matters of art on the Pacific coast. By the time Isadora was four months old, he had deserted the family, wandering the streets disguised as a woman to evade his creditors.

Isadora's mother moved with her children to Oakland, California, where she eked out a living giving piano lessons. By the time Isadora was six, she, too, was teaching—she taught "dance" to a bunch of toddlers. Her method was already original. The children practiced sitting, waving their arms, standing, opening doors, kneeling, and turning, until beautiful, simple movement became second nature to them. It was the beginning of Isadora's lifelong commitment to change dance and educate the young.

inspired by nature

By age eleven, Isadora had dropped out of school (her mother thought all schooling could be gotten from books) and was running a dance academy with her older sister, Elizabeth.

"I followed my fantasy and improvised," Isadora once said, "teaching any pretty thing that came into my head." She was inspired by the wind, the waves, the redwoods, and, most of all, Greek myths.

The Duncan children all gave public performances of dances and skits they wrote themselves. Isadora burned with a passion for art and for truth. She refused to let traditions confine her. Ballet, she felt, was a prison for the body. It consisted of rigid motions that were unnatural. Popular dances, with routine dance steps, were crude. At eighteen, she decided to go to Chicago and present her own kind of dance. Her family went with her. But Chicago offered her no opportunities. Finally, she landed a spot with a touring theater company based in New York City in 1895.

classical ballet at the end of the nineteenth century

When Isadora Duncan began dancing in public, audiences were used to watching classical ballet performed by formally trained dancers. Their movements were rigidly structured, and so were their costumes. Ballerinas wore ballet slippers that bound their feet tightly to make their movements look more mechanical. Duncan would reject every part of classical ballet, which she called "sterile gymnastics."

performing for new york society

For two years, Isadora toured with the company, painfully aware that she was wasting her genius. "What's the good of having me here," she asked the producer, "when you make no use of me?"

She began performing regularly in private living rooms for wealthy art lovers. She danced barefoot, wearing loose tunics, like the clothing depicted on Greek statues. Her costume alone was shocking to many people. At that time, proper women wore stiff full-body corsets under layers of clothing that covered nearly every inch of their bodies. But to be shocking was to be interesting!

Still, Duncan did not feel fulfilled. New York, she said, gave "no intelligent sympathy or help for my ideas." Her huge ambition drove her forward.

Dance at the turn of the twentieth century ranged from tap dancing in vaudeville theaters to ballet, most of it following well-worn conventions. Only Isadora was saying that movement could express a spiritual truth. Only Isadora thought dance should represent the deepest self of the dancer without imitating anything else. She was presenting the origin of pure movement and believed in it from the depths of her soul.

vaudeville

As the twentieth century was dawning, people hungry for entertainment flocked to theaters to see vaudeville shows. These were variety performances that included a range of acts from singers, dancers, and comedians, to jugglers, magicians, and dog tricks. Vaudeville began to decline as the theaters started to show moving pictures.

Audiences had never seen a woman drift, prance, and twirl about the stage trailing lengths of fabric as Isadora Duncan did. Many were shocked. Even when she danced to the music of revered composers, some critics protested that classical music should not be accompanied by what seemed to some to be aimless posturing in a seminude state. By now she was known by her first name alone: Isadora.

escaping to europe

Isadora decided American audiences could never appreciate her. With contributions from her society supporters, she and her family set sail for London.

She and her brother Raymond spent hours studying the Greek statues in the British Museum. She performed at the Royal Court Theater, dressed in a flowing tunic and barefoot on a bare stage, with only a piano and a dark blue backdrop. Stark and dramatic, it became her signature act.

London had enlarged her ideas. But she still felt unappreciated. Raymond had gone to Paris. He urged Isadora and her mother to follow him. They went.

to paris

It was 1900, the year of the Paris Exposition Universelle, where people first saw talking films, escalators, and diesel engines. Degas, Manet, and Rodin were a few of the artists who made the city the epitome of art and the showcase for the new.

Isadora and her family rented a studio apartment, and there she stood for hours before a mirror, studying her body, looking for the "central spring of all movement." For a ballet dancer, all movement came from the center of the back, at the base of the spine. But following this method made a dancer's steps artificial, like a puppet's. No, she decided, the "central spring" came from a source inside: the solar plexus, a spot just below one's ribs.

Isadora's performances were radically different from anything seen in Paris before, and they quickly captured people's attention. A fascinated Rodin came to sketch her. The sculptor Bourdelle created statues modeled on poses from her dances for the facade of a new theater.

The reigning queen of performance in Paris was Loie Fuller, whose vigorous novelty "dance" with colored scarves was a music hall sensation. Fuller was intrigued by Isadora and invited her to join her 1902 tour of Europe. Isadora readily accepted. In Vienna, she was called "the naked nymph." In Berlin, she told journalists that a dancer should move according to her nature, as all animals do. In the future, she said, no dancer would move as they did in ballet and popular performances, but "in the form of a woman in her greatest and purest expression . . . bringing to the world the thoughts and aspirations of thousands of women. She shall dance the future of woman." It was the giant ambition of a genius.

Leaving Fuller's company, Isadora packed up her family again—and went on a pilgrimage to Greece. They toured the Acropolis dressed as ancient Greeks and selected a site for a Duncan family temple, a temple that was never built.

a school for the duncan method

All the while, Isadora was determined to start a school. She needed followers to carry on her style. In 1905, she selected the town of Grunewald in Germany and recruited twenty children from poor neighborhoods. The little students received free tuition, room, and board. They were taught that the foundation of all other studies was dance.

When she was in Grunewald, Isadora would burst into the school and cry, "What is the greatest thing in life?" The children would chorus, "Love!" Her much more severe sister, Elizabeth, ran the school. Six of the most talented little girls were specially trained to perform with Isadora and became famous around the world as the "Isadorables."

With a school and her entire family to support, Isadora had to go on touring. She had begun a relationship with Gordon Craig. They had a child, a girl named Deirdre, whom Isadora cherished.

the meteor returns

In 1908 Isadora made a triumphant return to the United States. In New York, her performances at Carnegie Hall and the Metropolitan Opera were sold out. President Teddy Roosevelt pronounced her "innocent as a child in a garden." Around the country, people remarked wonderingly that she danced with her whole body. A reviewer said her body seemed bewitched by the music.

tragedy strikes the first time

On April 19, 1913, she was back in Paris. She had achieved great success. Every dream of her youth was coming true. She had taken up with the heir to the Singer Sewing Machine fortune and had a son, Patrick, with him. Life was as perfect as it could be.

That afternoon, Isadora's two beautiful young children were put into a hired car to go to their hotel for a nap. The car stalled. Getting out to crank the starter, the driver forgot to apply the hand brake. He watched helplessly as the car shot forward and sank into the Seine River. Onlookers dove in to save the children and their nurse, but all of them drowned.

Isadora suffered such agonizing grief, her friends thought she would never dance again. Her bright red hair turned white. But within a year she had started a new school in Paris, this time for boys as well as girls. And she toured with her Isadorables.

The times were changing and so were people's tastes. Ragtime music became popular after World War I, as did new dances like the foxtrot and tango. Artists no longer looked to Greece for inspiration. One country was enthusiastic about Isadora, however: the Soviet Union. Isadora was invited to Moscow by the young Soviet government, which sponsored a school for her in 1921. When she returned to the United States, she ran into intense anti-Communist feeling. Suspicious officials interrogated her for hours before they would let her into the country.

final tragedy

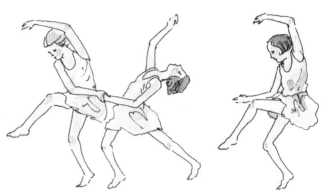

Isadora was past her prime and noticeably plump. "It's terrible that God gave me the secret of beauty . . . and yet I no longer have the power to give it to the world. It's all there inside me . . . waiting to come out," she lamented.

She returned to Europe. A friend gave her a long red shawl, and she wore it everywhere. On September 14, 1927, on the Riviera, Isadora climbed into a two-seater sports car. Throwing her shawl over her shoulder, she gaily cried, *"Je vais à l'amour"* (*I go to love*). As the car lurched forward, the end of her scarf caught in the spokes of a wheel, pulled tight, and broke Isadora's neck.

Her dances live on. The six Isadorables had changed their last names to Duncan. Now they carried on Isadora's work. She had changed dance forever. The effects of her beliefs and practices live on—both in how dancers move and how women see themselves and their bodies.

"I was never able to understand . . . why, if one wanted to do a thing, one should not do it. For I have never waited to do as I wished."

—isadora duncan

MARGARET SANGER

*crusader for women's
reproductive freedom*

1879–1966

Margaret Sanger's campaign for women's reproductive health freed working-class families from having more babies than they could support and care for. She knew the hardship firsthand: Her mother was pregnant eighteen times and died young. When Sanger began her work, advocating for birth control—a term she coined—was against the law. It was illegal just to share information about it. Sanger defied the law and landed in jail. She emerged even more determined to succeed. By establishing clinics to educate poor and immigrant women about their bodies, she saved lives, reduced poverty and domestic abuse, and opened the way for married women to pursue careers. Late in her life, Sanger was the driving force behind the development of a birth control pill.

margaret "maggie" louise higgins was born in

1879 in Corning, New York, where her Irish father, Michael, was a stonecutter who specialized in angels and wreaths for tombstones. He was often out of work, and every two years or so his large family had to move from one rundown home to another. Maggie remembered her father, who championed worker's rights and socialism, as a radical democrat who was kind to strangers and those less fortunate. Maggie's mother had eleven babies from eighteen pregnancies. Her mother was dead at forty-eight, while her father lived to be eighty.

leaving a troubled home

As business dried up and food became scarce, the older Sanger children found jobs in nearby factories. Left at home when she was eight, Maggie cared for four younger siblings, did most of the housework, and took in laundry for pay. She was as feisty as her bright red hair made her look. She was proud of the Higgins family's reputation as rebel outsiders.

Maggie's older sisters pooled their money to pay her tuition at a boarding school a few hours from home. They wanted to save her from having to work as a maid or laundress or to marry a factory worker. She found herself among a group of privileged young people. While she worked in the kitchen to pay for expenses, she dreamed of going to medical school.

But the money ran out again, and Maggie dropped out to teach school. When a sister wrote that their mother was dying of tuberculosis, Maggie rushed home to nurse her until the end. Women like her mother had no reliable way to prevent pregnancies. Too many could ruin a woman's health, as they ruined that of Maggie's mother.

Maggie still wanted to become a doctor, but the family had no money for medical school. The field of nursing was rapidly expanding, and the training period was much shorter. So she enrolled in a nursing program, specializing in a field that, from helping her mother, she already knew something about: obstetrics and gynecology. Before long she had developed a chronic cough and such fatigue she could hardly rise from her bed. She had caught her mother's tuberculosis. It would plague her for many years.

marriage to will sanger

Even with a chronic illness, Maggie was fiery, fun-loving, sensual, fiercely intelligent. She longed for work and, as she once said, a "world of action." But several men came courting, and one managed to overcome her doubts about marriage: Will Sanger, an aspiring architect. She accepted his proposal, marrying him in 1902 and graduating with a nursing degree the same year.

Maggie and Will moved in with his parents in New York City. Soon she became pregnant. Worried that her tuberculosis was a danger to the baby, she went for treatment to a sanitarium at Saranac Lake. A healthy baby son was born in 1911. The little family went to live in the "dream house" Will had designed and built for them in the suburb of Hastings-on-Hudson.

finding her calling

After having two more babies, Maggie Sanger had reached the limit of her tolerance for homebound life. She needed to be helping people. Will was tired of working for other architects. They decided to move back to New York City.

In the city, Will and Maggie saw the poor being oppressed by powerful, moneyed interests. In Greenwich Village, they found socialist thinkers who agreed with them. Many were fighting against income inequality and for women's right to vote. Emma Goldman, a radical political activist and writer, preached "free love" as a way to end the traditional patriarchal marriage, which she called an economic arrangement. Women should be able to find love outside of a marriage agreement, she added.

greenwich village radicals

Greenwich Village—"the Village"—is a neighborhood in Lower Manhattan that has long been a home to artists, musicians, writers, and free thinkers.

The Sangers mingled with social critics Max Eastman and John Reed, whose calls for a political revolution appeared in a publication called *The Masses*. Writer Upton Sinclair argued in the Village's clubs about the need for social reform, while the wealthy Mabel Dodge hosted artists and writers, including Emma Goldman and labor organizer Bill Haywood, at her Fifth Avenue apartment.

Maggie Sanger began speaking up in meetings about women's traditional duty to raise healthy, moral children. Yet when the moral children were grown, they entered a greedy and corrupt society. Sanger declared that women's first duty was to change society.

The radical bohemians of Greenwich Village were impressed by this vital young nurse. One night, at a rally for the poor, she was asked to speak. Sanger chose to address society's unwillingness to support women's reproductive health. Women had no way to protect themselves from unwanted pregnancies. Having many babies prevented women from earning an income. Too many mouths to feed kept whole families forever destitute.

When she had finished, many listeners wanted desperately to know how rich women limited their families. Sanger's answers were so clear and powerful that her colleagues asked her to publish them in a socialist magazine.

When the magazine came out, the pages devoted to her article were blank— they'd been censored. It was a crime to print anything on birth control or to send the information through the mail. Sanger was incensed. The law was killing women.

the comstock act

In 1873, the US Congress passed the Comstock Act to prevent "trade in, and circulation of, obscene literature and articles of immoral use." The law was named after a crusader named Anthony Comstock, who created the New York Society for the Suppression of Vice. Comstock was concerned that women would put careers ahead of having children and pressured Congress to make it illegal to sell or distribute information about birth control. Not until 1971 did Congress remove the language from the act preventing information about contraception to be shared.

sadie sachs ignites a cause

Sanger worked in New York as a visiting nurse. She paid visits to immigrant women living in run-down tenements on the Lower East Side. One day in 1912 she was called to Grand Street. There, Sadie Sachs lay unconscious with her anxious husband, Jake, at her bedside. The couple already had three children and could not afford to have any more. Sadie had undergone a five-dollar abortion that had gone wrong. Sanger was barely able to save her, but she did.

Three months later, Sadie was pregnant again. In desperation, she tried to end the pregnancy. Sanger rushed to her side, but this time Sadie died. Sanger walked the streets, tormented by the scene she had just left. That starry night gave birth to a crusade. "I was resolved to . . . change the destiny of mothers whose miseries were vast as the sky," Sanger later wrote.

the battle begins

Sanger launched a campaign to educate the public about limiting pregnancies, publishing articles titled "What Every Mother Should Know" and "What Every Girl Should Know." She frankly said that sex was necessary to a woman's health, because it was so essential a part of her physical makeup, but warned girls to delay it until they were in love. Unwanted pregnancies kept families poor, and kept women from working.

Articles might be persuasive, but they weren't enough. Emma Goldman and other radical friends taught Sanger how to organize people and go after a goal. In 1914, Sanger started a monthly paper, *The Woman Rebel*. In it she published all the information she could about what she called "birth control." Because her articles broke Comstock's law, she was arrested. Rather than go to jail, Sanger fled to London.

There, she befriended British radical thinkers, including Havelock Ellis, one of the first philosophers to write frankly about sex. She also went to a clinic in Holland to learn about their methods of contraception. Sanger became more convinced than ever that her crusade could change women's lives in the most profound ways. Women had to be able to control their own bodies and decide when they wanted to have babies if they were to be free. Freedom would mean that relations between men and women could be equal.

Back in New York, Will Sanger openly distributed his wife's pamphlet *Family Limitation* and was put in prison. Maggie hurried home from Europe. Days after she returned, her youngest child, five-year-old Peggy, died of pneumonia. The loss was almost more than Sanger could bear. She had left her children behind when she fled the country. Now she was tormented by guilt.

She had long wanted to end her marriage to Will, but he would not agree to it. As they both mourned the loss of their daughter, Will persuaded Maggie to go to Paris with the family so that he could paint there. She agreed, intending to find out French methods of contraception. She didn't stay there for long. For her, the marriage was over. Leaving Will and the children behind, she returned to New York, hiding in her corset the contraceptive devices she'd been given by French women.

birth control for the masses

On October 16, 1916, Sanger opened her first clinic in Brownsville in Brooklyn, New York, circulating a flyer printed in English, Italian, and Yiddish. It offered women instruction in the use of birth control devices.

More than one hundred women lined up on the street even before the door opened. Sanger and her sister, a fellow nurse, explained birth control and where to buy the devices. On the ninth day, a woman demanding immediate attention turned out to be a detective. She arrested Sanger for again violating the law against sharing information about birth control.

This time, Sanger spent thirty days in prison. The resulting publicity stirred interest in her campaign. She founded a journal called *The Birth Control Review* and edited it until 1929. She wrote numerous books and traveled around the world lecturing about birth control. In 1922, backed by people who believed in her message, she founded the American Birth Control League.

By 1930, Sanger's Birth Control League operated fifty-five clinics in twenty-three cities. Her most powerful adversary was the Catholic Church, which called contraception worse than abortion. But the church couldn't stop the movement Sanger had launched.

In 1932, after Sanger helped file a lawsuit, a court finally ruled that it was legal to distribute birth control information through the mail. This opened the way for the American Medical Association to label birth control as preventive medicine. Doctors were free to prescribe it. It was finally legal for families to choose when to have children.

By 1942, Sanger had remarried and was living in retirement in Arizona. The league of birth control clinics she had founded changed its name to Planned Parenthood.

the pill

Sanger had not given up on finding a contraceptive that would be reliable and easy to use. In 1952, she met Dr. Gregory Pincus, who researched fertility at Worcester University in Massachusetts. The two decided to pursue development of a birth control pill.

Because Planned Parenthood offered only lukewarm support, a frustrated Sanger persuaded her friend Katharine McCormick, heir to the McCormick reaper-machine fortune, to contribute a substantial sum to Pincus.

When the time came for human trials of the pill, Dr. John Rock of Brookline, Massachusetts, came on board and tested the method. In 1960, the Federal Drug Administration approved the pill for contraception.

For the first time in history, women could truly control their bodies and plan families, giving them a footing in many ways equal to that of men. Almost instantly "the Pill" started a sexual revolution from which there was no return.

Margaret Sanger died in 1966, months after a US Supreme Court decision made birth control legal for married couples. Her lifelong crusade liberated women. Planned Parenthood is still the foremost, and in some places the only, organization around the world that promotes family planning and healthy sex lives for women.

Sanger's association with the eugenics movement, which aimed to purify society by preventing the "defective" from reproducing, has sullied her legacy. Sanger had helplessly witnessed the misery of families too disadvantaged to care for their large numbers of children. That may help to explain her involvement, but certainly doesn't excuse it.

However, some of the attacks on her cannot be justified. In 1921, Sanger referred in writing to her fear that she'd be accused of wanting to "exterminate" the "Negro race" with her birth control campaign. Some opponents of Planned Parenthood have seized on that word to twist her meaning and accuse her of deadly racism. In accepting the Margaret Sanger Award in 1966, Dr. Martin Luther King Jr. said, "There is a striking kinship between our movement and Margaret Sanger's early efforts. . . . Margaret Sanger had to commit what was then called a crime in order to enrich humanity, and today we honor her courage and vision."

*"No woman can call herself free
who cannot choose the time to be
a mother or not as she sees fit."*

—margaret sanger

ETHEL PERCY ANDRUS

changing the face of aging

1881–1967

Ethel Percy Andrus, a visionary educator, inspired Americans of all ages to improve life for others. As one of the first woman high school principals in California, Andrus helped her students develop character and skills by involving them in community service. Much later in life, she founded a nonprofit membership organization called the American Association of Retired Persons (later renamed AARP) so that older members of society could achieve greater meaning and purpose. Andrus's vision was to focus on living, not aging, and to embrace the later years as a time for personal growth and community participation. Under her leadership, AARP became a powerful force for better health care, greater financial security, and personal fulfillment for all of us as we age.

ethel percy andrus was born in San Francisco on September 21, 1881, to an idealistic young lawyer and his wife. In 1890, she, her parents, and her older sister, Maud, moved to Chicago, where her father continued his legal studies.

Andrus's parents believed in serving others. This value became the centerpiece of her life. As an adult, she reflected on her "conviction that we must give of ourselves, to our fellows—to do some good, somewhere, for which we would receive no pay other than the satisfaction of doing."

learning to serve

A confident, brilliant girl, Andrus graduated from Austin High School with honors and earned a bachelor's degree from the University of Chicago. From 1903 to 1910, she taught English and German at the Lewis Institute (now the Illinois Institute of Technology). During her free time, she volunteered by teaching classes to the poor at Hull House, the settlement house founded by Jane Addams to help immigrants and local residents build skills to achieve happy, secure lives. It changed Andrus to watch them study English, adapt to their new circumstances, acquire new skills, and be given a place where they could practice the arts. "I learned there to know life intimately and to value folks of different races and creeds," she said. Together, teaching and volunteering made her life fulfilling and complete.

But her father's failing health took the family back to California in 1909. After teaching high school for several years, she was hired as assistant principal at Abraham Lincoln High School. The neighborhood had once been affluent but was changing. Most of the students came from poor families and reflected many nationalities, including Chinese, Japanese, Russian, Italian, and Mexican.

After only a few months, the principal retired and Andrus replaced him, becoming the first woman to serve as principal of an urban high school in California. She faced unique challenges, including one of the highest dropout and delinquency rates in the country.

a community of many nations

One of the first things Andrus did as Lincoln's principal was spell out the word OPPORTUNITY in big letters over the school's entrance gate. She set out to shape the many different populations of the school—and the town—into one cosmopolitan community dedicated to excellence. Everyone began to feel pride in the school, in each family's roots and traditions, and in their shared American citizenship.

Every school day began with all present reciting a pledge that included: "I hold these truths to be self-evident: that all men are created equal. God hath made of one blood all races of men, and we are his children, brothers and sisters all." Andrus carried out her bold reforms with motherly warmth. "I never met a child who couldn't embrace me," she once said. She stood firm for discipline, personal responsibility, and pride in accomplishment.

In 1919, Andrus helped get the neighborhood renamed Lincoln Heights, to further instill pride in its residents. The school was soon nationally recognized for its excellence. Andrus set an example as a student herself. She earned a master's degree in 1928 and a PhD in 1930 from the University of Southern California.

Drawing on her experience at Hull House in Chicago, Andrus organized Lincoln High students into ambitious service programs that reached every corner of the community.

"Youth, like age, wants to be needed, to be praised, and be a member of a team," she wrote.

Students worked in hospitals as nurses' aides, ran errands for homebound residents, supervised playgrounds for younger children, made furniture for civic organizations, and formed art classes to make posters for local events. Recognizing the desire for education among her students' immigrant parents, she set up evening courses called the Opportunity School for Adults. She recruited plumbers, preachers, engineers, and upholsterers to teach classes. Their collective efforts brought the community together and helped pull people out of poverty.

Delinquency declined so much, the courts gave her a citation for her success in reducing crime by young people. "Somehow, you found yourself acting the way she wanted you to," said a former student.

In 1944, her mother's health began to fail rapidly. Andrus immediately resigned from Lincoln High to care for her.

After recovering, Andrus's mother encouraged her daughter to turn her attention to the needs of older people—who had to keep working at something worthwhile, she said. And when they got too old to work, they needed to know someone cared about them. Andrus realized that her mother was right.

the chicken coop

She went to work as a volunteer for the Association of California Secondary School Principals, serving on a committee addressing retired teachers' living conditions.

One day, she received a call from a local grocer asking her to check up on an older woman who needed help. She went to the address the grocer gave her and was surprised to find a sizable, well-kept house. A neighbor recalled an old woman who lived out back. That's when Andrus discovered that a retired teacher was living in a windowless chicken coop. A woman in shabby clothes came out of it, too proud to let her visitor see inside. She had been a

Spanish teacher and had lost her savings in the Depression. She lived on her forty-dollars-a-month pension—too meager to cover proper housing, health care, and food.

The woman still had spirit and didn't feel like a victim. But she needed to be part of a community and she needed services that would make her secure and restore her dignity.

Andrus knew an individual voice wasn't very loud. But a number of voices, all asking for the same thing, got attention. To boost the collective voices of retired educators, she founded the National Retired Teachers Association (NRTA) in 1947.

the power of numbers

Inspired by the woman in the chicken coop, Andrus sought to create an experimental community where retired teachers could live with dignity and purpose. She envisioned a place where people were not isolated or lonely. Activities could include swimming pools, gardens, fitness, and art centers, to be sponsored by the NRTA. It was a radical idea. At the time, few such places with services and amenities existed except for the very rich.

This dream became a reality in 1954, after Andrus persuaded officials in the small village of Ojai, California (about eighty miles northwest of Los Angeles), to let her buy the former Grey Gables Inn. She told them it would contribute to the community. Retired members would tutor in the schools, volunteer at the public library, and serve in many other ways. Filled with healthy, active retired teachers, Grey Gables became a model for the future of retirement communities in the United States. The town of Ojai would later issue a proclamation honoring Grey Gables's contributions to the community.

Another top priority was finding health insurance. At the time, most workers were required to retire at age sixty-five, and no companies would sell them health insurance they could afford. Andrus went to forty-two insurance companies with a proposal for a group policy. All forty-two companies turned her down. "They thought I was a crank," she said, but she refused to give up.

Several years later, Andrus finally found an insurance broker who would write policies for her retired teachers. The new health plan was an instant success, attracting more and more members and allowing them to afford health insurance despite being past sixty-five. Other retirees clamored for the same benefits.

In 1958, Andrus and several trusted advisors drew up plans for an organization for all retired people, not just former teachers. They called it the American Association of Retired Persons. The new organization published a magazine, *Modern Maturity*. Ethel Percy Andrus was its editor and wrote its eloquent editorials.

She wrote and spoke frequently about a "new image of old age"—describing older persons as zestful, energetic, and wise. Andrus fought against age-based discrimination, quoting politician and activist Oscar Ewing, who noted, "This is a country where it is wonderful to be young. It must also become a country where it is wonderful to be old."

To help people envision how to grow older at home, Andrus worked with the building industry to construct a model home that featured no stairs, grab bars in the bathrooms, nonskid flooring, and other safety features. This 1961 "House of Freedom" in Washington, DC, was way ahead of its time.

Ever the educator, Andrus created the Institute of Lifetime Learning to promote continuing education. Through classes in several cities, informative articles in *Modern Maturity*, and even record albums, millions of older adults learned about history, geography, art, science, and more.

AARP also added a prescription-medicine program, group travel programs, and discounts on a wide range of other products and services. By organizing retired consumers, AARP transformed the marketplace, persuading businesses that older people were valuable customers.

leading the millions

Andrus led the NRTA and the rapidly growing AARP. Her editorials inspired readers to see retirement as an opportunity to serve others and find fulfillment. She urged people to get a part-time job, volunteer in the community, fight for civil rights, take a course, make something, travel—in other words, continue to grow and make a positive difference in their community.

Andrus also traveled the country to meet retirees and speak to them face-to-face. She was a respected advocate in Congress for lower prescription drug prices, affordable health care, and financial security for people as they aged. For months at a time she lived out of her suitcase. People noticed that when she entered a room full of chattering people, everyone went quiet. Andrus inspired awe. She was never paid for any of her work.

Ethel Percy Andrus died in July 1967. Because of her work, aging has taken on a fresh, dynamic meaning. AARP, with nearly thirty-eight million members, continues to empower people to choose how they live as they grow older. Through her vision and passion, Ethel Percy Andrus inspired young people to serve and grow, and encouraged generations of people to create a brighter future as "the architects of our added years."

hard to imagine, but . . .

Before Andrus founded AARP, most businesses required workers to retire when they reached the age of sixty-five. Upon retirement, 75 percent lived with their children because they were too poor to afford independent living. Insurance companies considered that older drivers posed the same risk as drunk ones and denied coverage. Older people were not expected to contribute any longer to society. As Andrus put it, they counted the days until they died.

"Old age is not a defeat but a victory, not a punishment but a privilege."

–ethel percy andrus

DOROTHEA LANGE

eloquent eye on a hidden america

1895–1965

During the 1930s, when the Great Depression nearly broke the spirit of America, Dorothea Lange took a photograph of a hungry, desperate woman. Called Migrant Mother, it is one of the most recognized pictures in the world. Dorothea Lange humanized documentary photography.
Her Depression pictures helped Americans empathize with victims of the economic collapse, who were otherwise invisible or overlooked. Her camera was an instrument for social justice, and her photographs are works of art.

She was born **dorothea nutzhorn** on May 26, 1895, in Hoboken, New Jersey. Her parents were upper-middle-class German immigrants—her father a lawyer, her mother a librarian. Theirs was a home filled with books, music, and talk of politics and history. During her earliest years, the family was a happy one. But that happiness ended so suddenly, Dorothea was left with a wound that never healed.

two traumas

First, in 1902, when she was seven, Dorothea contracted polio. There was no cure. For months she had to wear heavy braces on her legs. Her right foot was disfigured and wouldn't flex properly. "[Polio] formed me, guided me, instructed me, helped me, and humiliated me," she later wrote.

polio

Polio (short for poliomyelitis) is an infectious disease that attacks the nervous system and can leave the patient with paralyzed muscles, often in one or more arms or legs. The majority of cases of polio occur in children under age five. Vaccines discovered in the mid-twentieth century have eliminated most polio cases around the world, though there is still no cure.

The second blow came when Dorothea was twelve. Without warning, her father disappeared, and she didn't see him for many years. Dorothea always said he deserted the family, and she never forgave him for it. In reality, he was fleeing people he owed money to, and Dorothea's mother continued to support him.

Dorothea, her brother, and their mother were evicted from their home and went to live with Dorothea's grandmother, a haughty woman given to alcohol-fueled rages.

Every day, mother and daughter rode the subway to the Lower East Side in Manhattan. Dorothea attended school there, and afterward roamed the streets until her mother's workday ended. On her own in the vibrant, diverse city, Dorothea learned to see. She loved the role of observer, imagining she wore what she called her "cloak of invisibility." By the time she was a teenager, all of Manhattan was her school. Dropping into a gallery, she saw the work of Alfred Stieglitz, who was making photography an accepted form of art. She sat in a theater where Isadora Duncan danced to Beethoven's Fifth Symphony. "To me it was the greatest thing that ever happened," she raved.

Her mother insisted that Dorothea be able to support herself. Teaching was one of the few options for a young woman at that time, so Dorothea enrolled in Columbia University's Teachers College. She had no intention of becoming a teacher, but in a remarkable stroke of luck, the great, poetic photographer Clarence White was teaching an extension course at the college. White's students were nearly all women, and he, unlike most men of the day, encouraged them to pursue careers if they showed talent. Dorothea clearly did.

To get practical experience, she applied for a job at Arnold Genthe's studio. He was the most eminent portrait photographer of the day. Dorothea learned every phase of making and developing photographs. Genthe, too, recognized Dorothea's talent and gave her a camera—her first.

westward bound

Seeing life as a learning opportunity, Dorothea and a friend decided to give themselves a very big life lesson: a trip around the world. They set off from New York City on a ship bound for New Orleans, then continued by train to California. San Francisco, rebuilt after a giant fire, was bustling and gleaming. Both young women felt right at home. But they hadn't been there very long when all their money was stolen. Rather than wire home for more, the two went looking for jobs. Dorothea found one developing photographs at a department store. Starting a new life in a new town, she shed her father's name, Nutzhorn, and took her mother's maiden one, Lange.

Vivacious, talented, and adventurous, she attracted many friends among San Francisco's bohemian artists. Her zest for life and her ambition made her exciting to be around. Before long, two wealthy gentlemen loaned her the money to open an elegantly designed portrait photography studio in the style of Arnold Genthe. She charged top rates and drew privileged customers. Naturally charismatic, she presented herself as freewheeling and stylish in flowing trousers and rakish hats. Soon she was mentioned in newspaper society columns.

family life

In 1920, Lange married Maynard Dixon, a noted painter whose subject was the Old West. It would be a turbulent marriage, with Maynard the pampered star. He would regularly disappear for weeks or months at a time to paint in Utah or Arizona, as he had always done. Lange worked hard, and soon her successful studio was supporting them both. They had two sons, born in 1925 and 1928.

With neither parent at home to care for the little boys, Dorothea reluctantly sent them to live with other families for long periods. As one of Lange's biographers has said, the boys both had a "store of bitter memories" of childhood, but they admired their mother.

her subject presents itself

The Great Depression, which began in 1929, transformed Lange's life and her photography. One day in 1932, looking down from her window, she noticed a jobless man wandering to and fro. He seemed to be acting out the helplessness of unemployment. No government program existed to create jobs. All of America was in crisis.

the great depression

The Great Depression was a global period of economic difficulty that lasted ten years. It began in October 1929, following the crash of the US stock market. Millions of people who had borrowed money to buy stocks lost the money after stock prices fell drastically. Banks failed. Companies laid off their workers. By 1933, the worst year of the Depression, about fifteen million Americans were out of work. In the Midwest, a plague of grasshoppers and then drought ruined farms and created a Dust Bowl. The Depression collapsed the US economy and spread around the world.

President Franklin D. Roosevelt (FDR), who had been elected in 1932, created economic programs called the New Deal that helped lift the country out of the Depression. Recovery didn't come until 1939, when manufacturing increased in response to World War II.

Dorothea had a camera. How could she continue to take flattering portraits of privileged people? "The discrepancy between what I was working on . . . and what I was seeing on the street was more than I could assimilate," she later said.

Dorothea took her camera down to the street. She photographed a man at a soup kitchen . . . a despairing worker with an overturned wheelbarrow . . . dockworkers striking over unfair hiring and bad pay. She had always sympathized with working people. Now she was focusing her camera on them.

Street photography called for a new technique. She had no light meter or built-in flash—neither had been invented. There was no uncertainty in a studio portrait. But photographing people on the street meant capturing fleeting, unpredictable moments. It took courage to invade her subjects' privacy. After all, these were not people asking for their portrait to be taken. It turned out very few ever objected.

The administration of Franklin D. Roosevelt began creating and expanding government programs to help all the Americans thrown out of work by the collapse of the economy. FDR's New Deal put people to work, making the government more effective, and thus strengthened the democratic ideals: government of the people, by the people, and for the people. Dorothea Lange was about to add unforgettable images to that effort.

her camera as a democratic instrument

FDR's Farm Security Administration was set up to aid the desperate rural population. Like the Works Progress Administration, another New Deal project that put people to work on building projects, it was hiring artists and writers to document its work. Lange joined them in 1935. That year, she ended her marriage to Maynard Dixon and began working with Paul Taylor, a progressive professor of economics. They interviewed migrant workers, and Dorothea illustrated Taylor's reports with powerful pictures. They were a brilliant team and soon fell in love and married.

Lange was superb at portraying members of the underclass. She believed that to do good work, she had to find common ground, and she found it by talking with them. She immortalized displaced farm families heading west in broken-down cars, desolate landscapes degraded by wind and drought, ironic billboards advertising the American Way.

Sometimes she included bosses and cops in the composition. "You can't do people in trouble without photographing people who are not in trouble, too," she later said, "because you have to have those contrasts."

Plenty of people believed that the poor were to blame for their own plight; that they were lazy or made stupid choices. Lange's pictures demonstrated how mean and naïve that view was.

When she and Taylor gave away her photographs to newspapers, Americans learned about a vast population of fellow citizens who had been left to try to survive, often in hopeless conditions. Her iconic *Migrant Mother* prompted emergency government action to prevent starvation in the woman's camp where it was taken. Lange wrote this of the picture: "I do not remember how I explained my presence or my camera to her, but I do remember she asked me no questions.

There she sat in that lean-to tent with her children huddled around her, and seemed to know that my pictures might help her, and so she helped me. There was a sort of equality about it."

a widening lens

In 1936, Lange and Taylor visited plantations in the Mississippi Delta. "Earlier I had gotten at people through the ways they'd been torn loose, but now I got at them through the ways they were bound up," Lange said.

When World War II began, Japanese American citizens were put in camps out of fear that they might undermine the war effort from within. Lange's pictures of them show people with immense dignity in the most humiliating of circumstances. So clear was their message that the US Army impounded her photographs; they were not seen for thirty years.

japanese american internment camps

The bombing of Pearl Harbor by Japan in December 1941 marked the United States's entry into World War II. Shortly afterward, President Roosevelt ordered all Japanese Americans on the West Coast to report to internment camps to keep them from providing aid to the enemy Japanese forces. These primitive camps, enclosed in barbed wire, would eventually house over one hundred and ten thousand Japanese Americans for up to four years.

In the 1950s, Lange's health began to fail. She suffered from ulcers and post-polio syndrome, a little-understood disability. But she hardly ever stopped working. With the great landscape photographer Ansel Adams, she cofounded the magazine *Aperture*, and she taught at California Institute of the Arts. "Bring the viewer to your side . . ." she would tell students. "You have the power to increase his perceptions."

final years

Lange carried out assignments for *Life* magazine and traveled with Paul to Asia, Egypt, and South America as he analyzed rural problems and she photographed them. For a three-year stretch she was too sick to do any work. She and Paul gathered her sons and their children together to make up for the time when work had come first and family a distant second. And in quiet moments, she taught her many grandchildren how to see the world around them.

In 1964, doctors told her she had terminal cancer. It was a blow. She had felt her life was in balance, and there was more work to do.

Lange helped photographer Edward Steichen compile the exhibition *The Family of Man*. She managed to appear in two films about her life and to prepare a giant retrospective exhibition of her work for the Museum of Modern Art (MOMA). Working almost to her last hour, Lange died on October 11, 1965.

Three months later, her first retrospective opened at MOMA. "Truly great art such as Dorothea Lange's belongs . . . to all civilization," wrote a critic, adding that she was an artist who could "discover . . . new truths in the cause of man."

"A camera is a tool for learning how to see without a camera."

—dorothea lange

GLADYS
TANTAQUIDGEON

champion of native american culture

1899–2005

When Gladys Tantaquidgeon's life began, Native American culture had long been brutally suppressed in most of the United States. The Mohegans, Tantaquidgeon's tribe, had managed to remain on land they had occupied for many generations in Uncasville, Connecticut, and lived a traditional life that was invisible to all but their immediate non-Indian neighbors. Tantaquidgeon's aunt and two other elderly medicine women maintained sacred traditions, and they chose Gladys to be the vessel in which to preserve them. After becoming an anthropologist, she helped reverse government policies that hurt Native Americans, working with Indian nations to fight for social justice and revive crafts and customs that were sacred to them. Tantaquidgeon understood how important it is for history and tradition to "lift our imaginations above the land and sea and into the clouds."

gladys tantaquidgeon was born on June 15, 1899, on

Mohegan Hill above the Thames River in southeast Connecticut. This was the geographic heart of Mohegan tribal life, where members have always believed spirits watch over them. The Mohegan people are known as Woodlands Indians. Tantaquidgeons (the name means *he who travels fast*) were leaders for many generations, holding firm to their beliefs as white communities increasingly surrounded them.

shaped by history and tradition

Uncas, a *sachem* (leader) of the Mohegans in the seventeenth century, had realized his people had to make peace with the white settlers or perish. He made a treaty with the "pale strangers" in 1638. But white settlement gradually robbed the Mohegans of their land until they were concentrated in the area of the hill in present-day Uncasville.

The federal government threatened to remove the tribe in 1831. This was the time of the Trail of Tears—the forced removal of tribes from the southern states to Oklahoma. Gladys's ancestor Lucy Occom Tantaquidgeon and her daughter and granddaughter saved the homeland by declaring themselves a "Christianized" people. The two younger women donated a plot of land, long a sacred site, for a community church, which became the cultural center for the Mohegans.

The Tantaquidgeons, direct descendants of Sachem Uncas, were still prominent members of the community when Gladys was born just before the end of the nineteenth century. She was immersed from the start in ancient traditions. When she was a baby and her nails needed trimming, for instance, her mother, Harriet, bit rather than clipped them to ensure that Gladys would not become a thief. She cut Gladys's hair only when the moon waned, to thicken it, and turned the girl's shoes over at night to prevent bad dreams. She put her daughter to bed when the whip-poor-will bird called.

Harriet was an expert beader and quilter, and Gladys's father, John, was just as faithful to the sacred traditions. A farmer and stonemason, he also carved wooden bowls and wove baskets, showing Gladys how to make them out of plant materials she gathered from a certain spot on the north side of the hill.

a traditional childhood

Gladys was the middle of ten children (three died). She had a joyful, gifted, loving family who welcomed visitors, made music (her father played the violin and her mother the piano), danced, and told stories of past accomplishments, all the way back to the American Revolution and earlier. Their house sat at the intersection of many ancient paths.

When Gladys was only five, three elderly medicine women—one of them Gladys's aunt, Emma Fielding Baker, and another, Fidelia Fielding, the last speaker of their language—chose Gladys to be their storehouse of traditions. They and generations of "faith keepers" before them had helped the Mohegans to survive. They taught Gladys how to spot and gather medicinal herbs and how to create crafts to the highest standards. She learned about the *makiawisug*, or "little people," who protected the healing plants. The three wise women trusted young Gladys to carry on endangered traditions, but not the language itself. They were afraid she'd be punished by schoolteachers and missionaries for speaking it, as they had been.

the mohegan language

Fidelia Fielding (1827–1908) was the last fluent speaker of the Mohegan language. After she died, nearly one hundred years went by. Then her descendant, Stephanie Fielding, asked herself, "How can I resurrect my tribal language?" Using Fidelia's diaries and other documents, Stephanie Fielding began to reconstruct the Mohegan language, including its grammar and vocabulary, and created a Mohegan Dictionary in 2006.

Gladys went first to the local Indian school and then to one for whites in New London, where she was told there were no more Indians in Connecticut. That wasn't true, of course, but the tribe wasn't officially recognized by the US government and therefore had no civil rights.

While Gladys's education at the hands of the wise women was unusual, their roles as tribal leaders was not. Emma Fielding Baker represented the Mohegans before the all-white, all-male state legislature. The chief, or ceremonial leader, today is a woman, Dr. Lynn Malerba.

college

In 1904, young pioneer anthropologist Frank Speck, who had earlier interviewed Fidelia Fielding, returned to Uncasville to conduct more research into Mohegan traditions. He was struck by little Gladys's intelligence and spirit. She was clearly a worthy apprentice to the elder women. The Tantaquidgeons respected him, and when Gladys was eleven, he arranged for her to visit his family in Philadelphia. In later summers, she visited with the Specks at their summer home in Massachusetts. For all the excitement of experiencing so different an environment, Gladys found herself uncomfortably identified as "the Indian girl." But she met Indians from other Northeastern tribes through the Specks as well.

Speck became a professor of anthropology at the University of Pennsylvania—where he had been the first student to receive a PhD in that field. Tantaquidgeon was his assistant at twenty. Although she hadn't gone to high school, she attended classes at the university's teachers' college. She was well on her way to following Sachem Uncas's example of accepting the realities of white society while maintaining her own identity.

a working anthropologist

Together, Tantaquidgeon and Speck visited Eastern tribes, including the Abenaki and the Penobscot, during the 1920s. This was fieldwork; she was becoming an anthropologist, and most importantly, discovering that different Native American peoples shared certain beliefs.

Those beliefs were disparaged by many academics of the day who didn't question the superiority of European-based American culture and therefore were condescending toward Native Americans. In time, thanks in part to Tantaquidgeon, anthropologists would begin to seek out the old stories and spirit beliefs, no longer dismissing them as superstitions beneath their interest.

Working with Speck, Tantaquidgeon saw how the Cayuga and other tribes had adapted to removal from lands they had always occupied. She visited the remote Naskapi in northern Canada, who still observed traditions from before trade began with Europeans hundreds of years earlier. In many tribes, those traditions were taught only to select individuals and no one else, much as Tantaquidgeon had been schooled by her mentors in Uncasville. The keepers of tradition enjoyed special respect and bore great responsibilities.

among the yankton sioux

In 1934, newly elected President Franklin Delano Roosevelt appointed John Collier as commissioner of the agency that became the Bureau of Indian Affairs. A progressive reformer and admirer of Native American culture, Collier set out to remake federal policy toward Native Americans. He lobbied Congress to pass the Indian Reorganization Act (also known as the Wheeler-Howard Act) in 1934. It reorganized tribes, granting many self-government and an opportunity to be officially recognized as nations. Collier's "Indian New Deal" officially reversed the long policy of eradicating Native culture to force assimilation. He hired teams of anthropologists to implement the new programs. Gladys was one of them, working among the tribes of the Northeast to recover cultural traditions, provide education, and encourage self-government.

She did it so well that Collier assigned her to the most difficult problems the agency faced, those of the Yankton Sioux, who had lost much of their land in the Dakotas and were desperately poor. As their traditional way of life died away under pressure from the federal government, they suffered hunger, disease, and despair. Tantaquidgeon realized reorganization of the tribes wouldn't succeed if the agency simply dictated to the Sioux instead of giving them a say in their own future.

Tantaquidgeon moved in with the Yankton and other Sioux people on their reservations in South Dakota and experienced their brutal living conditions herself. The land they'd been forced onto was unsuitable for growing anything; they had little electricity, and sometimes no running water. Stores were more than eighty miles away. Assimilation had banned ceremonial dances and crafts, including the use of the sacred pipe. Gladys received a Sioux pipe for "safekeeping" and kept it hidden. In 2016, during the Sioux water protectors' action at Standing Rock, that pipe was returned as medicine to support the cause by a Mohegan delegation. Today, the Sioux speak Gladys's name whenever that pipe is lit.

The US government had long required Sioux children to be raised in Indian boarding schools. When they were returned to their families they were virtual strangers. Tantaquidgeon began teaching the parents, separated from their children for much of their lives, how to recreate family life. She also brought Native artists to several reservations to practice and teach forgotten craft culture, ceremonial dances, and other previously forbidden practices. As a result, people were able at last to support themselves economically and spiritually. She shared the belief with medicine men that when society is in balance, the old medicine (culture) will restore health.

home again

Tantaquidgeon was applying the lessons of her childhood as well as those of anthropologists. In 1938, Tantaquidgeon gave a radio talk in which she urged conservation of natural resources. "The Indian carefully guarded [nature's] gifts, and wastefulness was unknown," she said, offering an example to the United States that has yet to be followed.

Tantaquidgeon was doing crucial work with tribes in the West, but after nine years, she was longing for home. When her father became ill in 1947, she packed up and left for Connecticut. To her surprise, she found she was a celebrity. *Mademoiselle* magazine had run a feature on her, though the story referred to her as a "modern Indian," a patronizing term, she thought. It was a reminder that many white Americans remained ignorant of Native American culture.

In the late 1920s, Gladys's father and brother Harold, who had also worked with Speck, had begun planning the Tantaquidgeon Museum, which would celebrate Woodlands Indian culture. They built it of local granite fieldstone right on Church Hill in Uncasville. Local families all contributed their treasures. Speck and many chiefs from around New England and New York had come to the opening in 1931. When Gladys returned, she brought many of the gifts she had received during visits to so many different peoples in the West. The museum is still there and is the oldest Indian-owned-and-operated museum in the country.

Life on Mohegan Hill restored Tantaquidgeon's spirits. Into her seventies, her exercise regime included jumping rope with the children. She made braided rugs and did beading, and she enlarged the museum, which hosted thousands of visitors a year. Its mission was her mission: to bring hope to new generations, based on solid history.

Tantaquidgeon's academic contributions are many. She published a monograph on medicine of the Delaware Indians, helped write tribal constitutions, and lectured at colleges and universities. At a local women's prison, where she found striking similarities to the deprivation and grimness of some Indians' lives, she served as a librarian for many years and did much to improve conditions there as well.

The Mohegans began the process of applying for federal recognition in 1978. Although recognized by the British in 1638, the tribe's history had been lost to the ages. Now it had to prove its very existence. Gladys Tantaquidgeon had saved some 20,000 records of births, graduations, marriages, deaths, and correspondence, dating back decades, all stored in shoe boxes under her bed! She organized them to file as critical evidence with the application.

On March 7, 1994, recognition was granted. When the phone call came, a great cheer went up on Mohegan Hill. "What do we do next?" Gladys Tantaquidgeon asked. She answered her question with a saying she had heard from a Yankton Sioux: "Remember to take the best of what the white man has to offer . . . and use it to still be Indian."

Throughout her life, Tantaquidgeon received much recognition. She received honorary doctorates from the University of Connecticut and from Yale. She was honored with the Connecticut Education Association's Friend of Education Award, the National Organization for Women's Harriet Tubman Award, was named official Mohegan medicine woman, and was inducted into the Connecticut Women's Hall of Fame.

She supported her tribe's purchase of 240 acres of the original Mohegan settlement overlooking the Thames River, and in 1998, the buying back of the ancient village site associated with Sachem Uncas, which had been a state park.

a great legacy

There was a great celebration when Tantaquidgeon turned 100. At a joyful ceremony, she was thanked for winning civil rights for her people around the nation, ensuring good relations with non-Indian people, preserving the environment, advocating for social justice in the local prison, helping to end boarding schools for Indian children, preserving traditional herbal remedies and ceremonies, and passing on the old stories that are at the heart of Indian spiritual life.

Gladys Tantaquidgeon died on November 1, 2005, at age 106, having helped Native Americans across the nation recover their culture, their history, and their self-respect.

"What would the Old World historic shrines and scenes be without their traditions and classical associations? And what would the New World scenes be without their human traditions recited as the ancients knew them to lift our imaginations above the land and sea and into the clouds?"

—gladys tantaquidgeon

ELLA BAKER

*godmother of the
civil rights movement*

1903–1986

You've probably heard of Martin Luther King Jr., Rosa Parks, and Malcolm X. But few outside the movement for Black America's civil rights know the name of Ella Josephine Baker. For fifty years, Miss Baker, as she was always called, was a beacon of courage and determination for young and old. Working mostly behind the scenes, because that's where male leaders usually thought she belonged, she inspired and guided the women and men, and particularly the young people, who risked their lives for integration and equality.

ella baker was born on December 13, 1903, in Norfolk, Virginia, in the midst of the divided and violent "Jim Crow" era. The Jim Crow laws kept the South entirely segregated—split into Black and white—in neighborhoods, jobs, transportation, hotels, theaters, restaurants, and even at drinking fountains. Blacks were prevented from voting, so they had no way to change the laws. Most knew they'd better step aside for a white person to pass and bow their heads if they were spoken to. Thousands of Black people were lynched—murdered by mobs, often for made-up offenses.

jim crow laws

Jim Crow laws like these enforced segregation in different states:

"Marriages are void when one party is a white person and the other is possessed of one-eighth or more Negro, Japanese, or Chinese blood." —Nebraska, 1911

"Any . . . place of public entertainment . . . which is attended by both white and colored persons [shall] separate the white race and the colored race." —Virginia, 1926

"Separate free schools shall be established for the education of children of African descent; and it shall be unlawful for any colored child to attend any white school, or any white child to attend a colored school." —Missouri, 1929

Ella's relatives were fiercely proud of being Black. When Ella was about six, a white boy called her "nigger." She chased him for blocks, pelting him with stones. No one would treat her as inferior! The movement she later helped lead was nonviolent, but Ella Baker always believed in self-defense.

growing up black

Baker's grandfather, Mitchell Ross, and grandmother, Bet, had been slaves on a plantation in North Carolina. After the Civil War, her grandfather purchased a section of the plantation and divided it into lots for his relatives. Ella moved there with her mother when she was seven and grew up shielded from racism, surrounded by people who loved her.

The stories her grandparents told gave her confidence and a powerful desire to raise up her people. Strong women who believed in education were her models. You didn't talk back to Ella's mother. Her high standards inspired the scrappy little girl to excel. She was drawn to people of all kinds, and by the age of nine she was already delivering speeches in church meetings. Later in life her voice was described as that of a "stage actress."

Ella's mother sent her off to Shaw Academy and University in Raleigh, where she was always first in her class and a champion college debater. She staged protests, too, one against having to perform spirituals for visiting white dignitaries and another in favor of being allowed to walk on the campus with a male companion. Overcoming (or ignoring) limits placed on women would be a lifelong effort for her.

organizing the disorganized

Baker wanted to go to medical school, but there was no money for that. Instead, she moved to Harlem, in New York City, in 1927. It was a thrilling, jazzy neighborhood, alive with creativity and pride in the Black artists who contributed to the "Harlem Renaissance." There, Baker began soaking up ideas for how to make life fair and just for people left out of the nation's prosperity. She knew how important it was for them to experience equality.

She never wanted to be a teacher—one of the few jobs available to educated Black women—and instead took odd jobs like waitressing. That gave her time to visit libraries and talk to people on the street. She took courses on the history of labor and made friends with strong women working for social change. She was developing her own strategies for helping ordinary people help themselves, spurred on by her childhood community that shared and worked to make things better for everyone.

In 1931, Baker got the opportunity to put her ideas into practice when she was hired to organize youth groups around the city. Young people, she believed, should make changes rather than follow orders from their elders. So she encouraged democratic decisions. She became a familiar figure: carefully dressed in a suit, a pillbox hat on her head, a no-nonsense look on her face—and usually with a twinkle in her eyes. In 1940, the NAACP (National Association for the Advancement of Colored People), founded in 1909, hired Baker as assistant field secretary to help the local branches grow and be effective. The essential work of her life had begun. It took her to the heart of the South, where segregation was still violently enforced.

give people light

A lone Black woman traveling in the Jim Crow South was sometimes in mortal danger and always subject to indignities. Baker was hauled out of dining cars when there were no seats set aside for Blacks. She slept on benches in the open because it was safer than being alone in a room. She often went to a different city every day, recruiting new members and convincing them that people could empower themselves. She held leadership-training conferences—including one attended by civil rights pioneer Rosa Parks. Baker called her program Give Light and the People Will Find a Way. Parks would put it into effect in Montgomery a few years later, with her historic bus ride.

The NAACP's membership soared because of Baker's work, but the rigid male leadership supported top-down rule. Baker "refused to play the role of the silent helper to the prominent male leaders," says her biographer, Barbara Ransby, and she "was an assertive, outspoken woman of strong opinions." Her male colleagues found her "difficult." Frustrated, she resigned her position in 1946, but she stayed involved as a member.

Back in Harlem, she worked on various committees for the local New York City branch of the NAACP, and in 1952 was elected its first woman president. Through demonstrations, protests, and newspaper articles, she fought for school integration and against police brutality.

boycotts and sit-ins

Rosa Parks's refusal to give up her seat on a Montgomery bus on December 5, 1955, sparked a bus boycott. In January 1956, Baker cofounded In Friendship, a group that raised funds for activists who were hurting financially because of the boycott.

The boycott was hugely successful. For a year, fifty thousand Blacks in the city walked to work. It resulted in the desegregation of the Montgomery bus system. New local activists emerged from the struggle, just as Ella Baker hoped they would.

Their victory helped ignite the Civil Rights Movement. Baker returned to the South in 1957 to help organize the new Southern Christian Leadership Conference, or SCLC, dedicated to ending segregation nonviolently. She hoped it would be a grassroots movement, led by the brave people, mostly women, who boycotted the buses.

Instead, when the boycott became national news, the media focused attention on one man: the Reverend Martin Luther King Jr. He became the face and voice of SCLC. He and the other ministers who led SCLC had never worked on an equal basis with a woman, certainly never with one who dared to say no to them. Neither Baker nor Rosa Parks was given a central role.

But when SCLC decided to launch a voting drive called Crusade for Citizenship, the leadership realized that only Ella Baker had the skill and experience to organize it. She was named temporary director, and in that post she helped unite the different groups around the region, enforce nonviolence, and defend against white supremacists who were viciously fighting back.

SCLC needed a permanent director, but it wouldn't hire a woman, so Baker prepared to return to Harlem. Then, on February 1, 1960, four Black college students in Greensboro, North Carolina, sat down at a whites-only Woolworth's store lunch counter and refused to budge until they were served. After a few days, the store gave in and served them. The sit-ins spread like lightning around the South. To show solidarity, students in the North sat in at Woolworth's stores that weren't segregated. After a few months, Woolworth's changed its policy and began serving southern Blacks.

The youngsters' courage and sacrifice promised a new kind of leadership for Black liberation, not the paternalistic kind Baker had worked under previously. This was her dream come true. But the movement needed a united front, so she tried to bring young and old together by arranging a meeting at Shaw University over the Easter weekend of 1960. Martin Luther King Jr. was the star attraction, and he spoke stirringly in a general session. When young people broke into small discussion groups, Baker made sure that southern students conducted their own discussions, so they wouldn't be overwhelmed by northerners' concerns. She and Howard Zinn, the historian, acted as adult advisors.

When the older SCLC leaders met, it became clear they intended to make the young protesters a junior auxiliary. Baker made sure that didn't happen. By the end of that weekend, a new independent Student Nonviolent Coordinating Committee, or SNCC, was founded, with Baker its executive director. Under her guidance, it was at the cutting edge of the civil rights struggle.

alphabet soup of civil rights groups in baker's time

NAACP—National Association for the Advancement of Colored People—founded by a group of prominent Black Americans in 1909 in response to lynchings and other violence

CORE—Congress of Racial Equality—founded in 1942 to fight segregation through nonviolent means

SCLC—Southern Christian Leadership Conference—founded in 1957 after the Montgomery bus boycott ended; its first president was the Reverend Martin Luther King Jr.

SNCC—Student Nonviolent Coordinating Committee— founded during a meeting chaired by Ella Baker in 1960; led voter-registration drives around the South

freedom and voting rights

In 1961, the northern-based civil rights group CORE sent white and Black students on Freedom Rides in public buses bound for the Deep South. They challenged segregation—persisting despite the Supreme Court's ruling that it was unconstitutional—on buses and at rest stops. The students were brutally beaten and the nation was shocked. SNCC stepped in to support the Freedom Riders. Ella Baker contacted the parents of those arrested and made sure they didn't lose their scholarships.

In 1963, the nation was shocked once again when peaceful demonstrations by men, women, and children in Birmingham, Alabama, were met with fire hoses, beatings, police dogs, and arrests. The demonstrators believed in their right to protest. Baker helped them organize in towns all over the South, calling her contacts and keeping everyone's spirits up.

She coordinated a huge voter-registration drive in Mississippi in 1964 as part of the Freedom Summer. Young John Lewis was one of the foot soldiers during Freedom Summer. When he found people picking cotton, he went out and picked alongside them. That was Baker's method of "local organized action," as opposed to "mobilization," where large crowds listened to charismatic speakers. She also helped to organize Freedom Schools, where hundreds of volunteers, white and Black, educated Mississippi students about civics and the Constitution. The schools followed Baker's philosophy: Every teacher a pupil, every pupil a teacher.

Also in 1964, when the Mississippi Democratic Party refused to include a million Black voters, Baker helped found the alternative Mississippi Freedom Democratic Party. The party demanded its delegates be seated at the national convention to choose a presidential candidate. Fannie Lou Hamer, a noted voting-rights activist, led the effort, which was broadcast on national television news. The Democrats finally offered seats to only two delegates. The new party rejected the offer. Baker negotiated a resolution: In the future, delegates would be chosen based on local populations—and half of them had to be women.

Ella Baker continued to teach and inspire young civil rights activists. She was a valued advisor to activists in a variety of causes, including the anti–Vietnam War effort and the Black Power and women's liberation movements. She was slowing down, but her young followers and admirers honored her often at meetings and banquets, and she spoke wisely of her decades of experience.

Baker died on December 13, 1986, her eighty-third birthday. Her memorial service in Harlem was packed with people of various races, faiths, beliefs, and classes, all devoted to her. She had been their guiding light.

ella's legacy

Ella Baker's nickname was Fundi, which comes from a Swahili word that means a person who passes down a craft to the next generation. She left behind the legacy of strong leaders whom she inspired and nurtured. In addition, the Ella Baker Center for Human Rights was named after her. "Following in her footsteps," its website explains, "we build the power of black, brown, and poor people to break the cycles of incarceration and poverty and make our communities safe, healthy, and strong."

"Until the killing of a black mother's son becomes as important as the killing of a white mother's son, we cannot rest."

—ella baker

GRACE
HOPPER

computer programming pioneer

1906–1992

Thanks to Grace Hopper, computers are everyday tools that all of us can use, even if we don't understand how they work. She was a thirty-seven-year-old professor of mathematics in the navy when she began working with the Mark I, the first computer. Because it had to help win World War II, Hopper learned how it worked in a hurry. After the war, while computer scientists concentrated on building bigger, more complex machines that mathematicians and engineers could use, Hopper realized that computers could be useful for everyone, if their software was easy enough for ordinary people to use. Her ideas for programming in simple English made computers essential in nearly everything we do.

grace murray's carefree childhood encouraged her native curiosity. She was born in a book-filled brownstone building in New York City on December 9, 1906. Her father was an insurance executive who used one of the first adding machines, and her mother was an amateur mathematician. Grace and her younger sister and brother attended excellent private schools and spent every summer at a family compound overflowing with cousins on a lake in Wolfeboro, New Hampshire. Once, when little Grace's canoe capsized, her mother grabbed a megaphone she kept handy and called from the shore, "Remember your great-grandfather the admiral!" This meant *Don't abandon ship!* Grace rescued her canoe and herself without help.

a budding engineer

Her parents also encouraged her interest in technology. When she was seven, Grace took an alarm clock apart. The contents scattered before she could memorize how they fit together, so she dismantled every clock in the house to find out. Her mother didn't reprimand her. She simply restricted her daughter's further experiments to one clock. Grace was learning to try things out and to persevere when her experiments failed.

She applied to Vassar College at sixteen and was humiliated when she didn't pass the Latin entrance exam and had to spend a year after high school studying the language. Once in college, she majored in physics and mathematics to prepare for an engineering career, although she didn't expect to find any jobs in the field for women. After graduating in 1928, she got her master's degree in mathematics from Yale, then began teaching math and a course on drawing and perspective at Vassar.

Her courses were tremendously popular. Blessed with a mischievous and creative sense of humor, she found new and entertaining ways to explain difficult concepts. When a math problem involved ballistics or weapons, she substituted the more exciting rockets and their trajectories. She insisted that her math students learn to write clearly and well, whatever they were studying.

Faculty members were permitted to take other courses at Vassar. Grace studied astronomy, biology, philosophy, and much else. As a polymath (a person who knows about many things), she would later insist that computers, which were at that time doing only math computations, could tackle any subject. She also studied for a PhD in mathematics from Yale.

In 1930, Grace married Vincent Foster Hopper, a graduate student in literature. He taught at New York University, so they commuted between New York City and Vassar, in Poughkeepsie, New York. Grace earned her PhD at Yale in 1934, the only woman to achieve the degree in mathematics that year. She then studied at the Courant Institute in New York, focusing on a mathematical concept called "finite differences."

pioneers in computing

The first automatic mechanical calculator was designed by Charles Babbage in the 1800s. He called it the "Difference Engine." Babbage also designed an Analytical Engine, which was programmed, as are modern computers. In Babbage's machine—as with adding machines and early modern computers—the programming took the form of cards with holes punched in them.

Babbage never completed his machines, but his friend Ada Byron Lovelace (1815–1852), a brilliant mathematician, translated an article about the Analytical Engine, adding a set of notes on how it worked and its future potential. She included a detailed explanation of how to do a particular complex calculation; that explanation is considered the first computer program. "She wrote the first loop," Hopper would say. "I will never forget. None of us ever will."

war brings a change in course

Hopper and her husband divorced during World War II, although Grace wore her wedding ring the rest of her life.

In December 1941, the Japanese attacked Pearl Harbor and the United States entered the war. Grace's ancestors had been navy men, and she was determined to carry on the tradition, despite being a woman. She tried to enlist and was rejected three times, because she was too old (at thirty-five), underweight (at 105 pounds), and needed as a teacher. She persisted, finally persuading the navy to take her in their Women's Reserves. After graduating from a crash course at the top of her class, she was posted to a mysterious basement at Harvard University.

This was Navy Commander and physicist Howard Aiken's pioneer computer lab. It housed his gigantic invention, the Mark I, which was a fifty-five-foot-long computer. Aiken gave Hopper one week to learn how to program it. "There was this large mass of machinery out there making a lot of racket," she remembered. "It was all bare, all open, and very noisy."

A team of mathematicians was to use the Mark I to predict how well various military operations would work. Once Hopper knew how to program the machine, Aiken told her she was going to write a book. She replied that she never had. He said, "You're in the navy now. You're writing a book." It was a manual for the Mark I. At 561 pages, it was the first computer manual.

In Hopper's records in the Computer History Museum in Mountain View, California, you'll find one dead moth taped to a sheet of paper. This artifact has been memorialized as the first computer bug, which was discovered one day in the Mark I. When an associate removed the insect, Hopper is supposed to have said, "You've debugged the computer." There are other examples of her sense of mischief. She kept a clock in her office with the numbers in reverse order.

Everything about computers was new, and much needed to be improved. Hopper wasn't very interested in the hardware. (She liked to say that it was the part of a computer "you could kick.") And although other kinds of computers were being developed elsewhere, Aiken and Hopper were thinking differently: They realized that the instructions for the machines—the software—were the future of computing. Those instructions, or computer code, had to be made easier to use.

a language for the computer

Hopper stayed at Harvard after the war, experimenting with ways the Mark I could be used for civilian purposes. In 1949, she went to work for the Eckert-Mauchly Computer Corporation in Philadelphia as a senior mathematician. The company had built BINAC, the first large-scale electronic computer—Mark I was mechanical, performing calculations using moving parts, as opposed to electronic microchips, as in contemporary devices— and Hopper wanted to be part of it.

Hopper hired a team that included many women and foreign-born technicians. The team was nicknamed the United Nations. She always stressed teamwork and gave credit to others for their ideas. She was a tough, down-to-earth boss known for her salty language, and her team loved her.

Hopper had to learn to program BINAC, but she didn't want to be limited by the systems currently being used—she could envision a better way to tell a computer what to do. In 1951, Hopper created the first *compiler*, a term she invented, which made programming much more efficient. It assigned a different shortcut code to a set of instructions, rather than having the programmer write all the instructions out every time. She gave a talk about it at a meeting of the Association for Computing Machinery. Hopper predicted that compilers would make computers important tools for ordinary people, since they no longer had to know all the instructions to make the computer work.

The talk received a skeptical response. "I had a running compiler," she later said, "and nobody would touch it because, they carefully told me, computers could only do arithmetic; they could not write programs. It was a selling job to get people to try it. I think with any new idea, because people are allergic to change, you have to get out and sell the idea."

Although many of the concepts in her talk are taught in high schools today, it took two years to get managers to accept her invention. But it was the revolutionary first step toward creating computer languages. Computing would become like driving a car—the driver doesn't need to know how to repair the engine. She also insisted that computer programs could be written in English. Letters were symbols, like numbers. Again, people resisted her new ideas. Hopper went ahead anyway. Her method was to proceed without permission from the boss; it was always easier to apologize afterward if she'd made a mistake. The result was a compiler called FLOW-MATIC, which used word commands instead of numerical codes, and could perform business tasks such as billing. Before her inventions, programmers had to remember a number that went with every instruction, so it was hard to learn and easy to make mistakes. She convinced people that they could be more productive if they wrote English-like instructions.

In 1956, at the time Hopper was perfecting FLOW-MATIC, the rival company IBM designed FORTRAN, the first true programming language. It made computing much easier and much faster, but each manufacturer had its own version. The US Defense Department was persuaded that *one* language was needed that would run on *any* computer. Hopper was an advisor to the committee that looked at models for a common language.

One was FLOW-MATIC. It provided the foundation for COBOL, the breakthrough "English-like" language and is still in use today. Hopper's compiler had opened a gate. Afterward, advances in programming flooded the field.

Hopper was recalled to active duty in 1967 to standardize COBOL for the navy. Her last nineteen years of work were performed wearing her crisp uniform. (It amused her to be sometimes mistaken for a stewardess or security guard.) Even after she retired for good in her eighties, she worked as a consultant for Digital Equipment Corporation, sharing her expertise.

hopper's legacy

Hopper was a visionary, always eager to move ahead. She saw that computer operation was about to grow exponentially and have limitless uses. She trained dozens of experts who fanned out over the industry, spreading her influence.

By the late 1970s, Hopper was telling colleagues that huge mainframe computers—computers that took up entire rooms, versus our small desktop and laptop computers today—were no longer necessary. A series of small linked machines could do big jobs just as well. She was in great demand as a lecturer, logging a hundred thousand air miles a year and living out of her suitcase. Her talks were imaginative and often very funny—she even made an appearance on the *Late Show with David Letterman*. Her last years were spent explaining how computers could be used in daily life.

She was the most recognized woman in mathematics in the twentieth century, with fifty honorary degrees from universities. She received the highest US Defense Department honor and the National Medal of Technology, presented by President George H. W. Bush in 1991, along with many other awards. When she died, on January 1, 1992, she was a rear admiral in the navy. A few years later, a new destroyer, the USS *Hopper*, was named after her.

"Humans are allergic to change. They love to say, 'We've always done it this way.' I try to fight that."

—grace murray hopper

RACHEL CARSON

defender of the environment

1907–1964

Rachel Carson is recognized as the founder of the modern ecology movement. Hers was the lone voice that first awakened Americans to the poisoning of the environment going on around them. Carson realized that widespread use of chemical pesticides to kill insects, weeds, and other pests was also killing helpful insects, birds, fish, trees, and the soil in which crops were grown, threatening human health. Her book Silent Spring, published in 1962, led to the creation of the US Environmental Protection Agency. Tragically, she died only eighteen months after Silent Spring came out.

rachel louise carson was born on a family farm in

Springdale, Pennsylvania, on May 27, 1907. The farm was not successful, and Rachel's older siblings all worked with their father at the local power plant. Her mother had to give up teaching when she married, so she was not allowed to fulfill herself in a career of her own. She poured all her love and ambition into Rachel, her youngest child. They shared a curiosity about and love of nature, spending long hours together outdoors, collecting specimens and attaching names to plants and flowers.

a born writer

Rachel devoured books and was soon writing stories. Her first nature story was published by *St. Nicholas Magazine*, a children's publication, when she had just turned fifteen.

After a childhood spent largely alone and with her mother, Rachel blossomed at a large regional high school. She played sports, engaged in social activities, and graduated at the top of her class.

To pay for Rachel's college, her mother sold the family silver and ran a farm stand. Still, there was only enough money to send Rachel to a nearby school. The Pennsylvania College for Women (now called Chatham University) provided women with an education equal to most men's. The writing professor recognized Rachel's gifts. Another professor, Mary Skinker, taught biology. A glamorous and compelling figure, she inspired great admiration in the undergraduates. Rachel switched her major to study with Skinker, who became her mentor and lifelong friend. Indeed, she changed the course of Rachel's life.

the world of waters

Skinker took a position at the Woods Hole Marine Biological Laboratory in Massachusetts. After graduating from college in 1929, Rachel Carson followed her there. She saw the ocean for the first time and was transformed. It awakened her gift for wonder and poetic description. She worked all summer in the lab surrounded by eminent scientists.

Rachel went on to Johns Hopkins University in Baltimore, Maryland, where she earned a graduate degree in marine biology.

Mary Skinker was now working for the government and urged Rachel to take the civil service exam, which was required for a government job. Carson scored higher than anyone else tested that year.

In an unlikely stroke of luck, she learned that the US Bureau of Fisheries needed scripts for a radio show it broadcast, and she was hired to write them in 1936. Her supervisor said one of her scripts was too good for the government, so Carson submitted it instead to the *Atlantic Magazine*. "Undersea" was a thrilling account of the creatures that live invisible to humans. Writing was her passion. In addition to her full-time work, Carson turned out regular nature columns for the *Baltimore Sun.*

the sea around us

Rachel shared her home with her mother, who managed their practical matters, in an arrangement that continued until her mother died. Carson also took in two nieces when her sister died unexpectedly—all while holding down her job. What she really longed to do was write, but circumstances made it nearly impossible to find time and solitude for it.

The publisher Simon & Schuster contacted Carson and asked her to expand the "Undersea" article into a book. Writing *Under the Sea Wind* took years, but on its publication in 1941, the book earned glowing reviews. Carson was hailed as a great new "woman naturalist." Sadly, because the United States had just entered World War II, few people cared to read about life under the ocean. Carson was devastated by the weak sales. Still, her ambition and her passion for marine biology drove her on.

She wrote a new book, *The Sea Around Us*, about the formation and populations of the world's oceans. The *New Yorker* published parts in serial form beginning in June 1951. The articles sparked tremendous interest in the book, which appeared that July to ecstatic reviews. Carson's approach—to describe the ocean's ecology and humanity's dependence on it—struck readers with force. She won the National Book Award and many other honors. Rachel Carson was suddenly a celebrity at forty-four. With a best seller, she finally had enough money to write full-time and to buy a cottage on the coast of Maine. Her new home would feed her soul and inspire her work for the rest of her life. To cap off her success, she acquired a snappy two-tone Buick car.

death sprays

In 1953, Carson and her Maine neighbor, Dorothy Freeman, began
a deep friendship that became the central relationship of Carson's life.
She felt that Freeman entered fully into the intellectual and creative
parts of her life and truly understood what she was trying to do with
her work.

The year 1957 brought another family claim on her emotions and
energy: Carson took over guardianship of her five-year-old grandnephew,
Roger. At the same time, her aging mother needed ever more care.

Still, Carson never stopped working. In 1958, a friend shared a letter she
had sent to the government protesting the spraying of pesticides to kill pests at
a bird sanctuary on Cape Cod. The sprays were supposedly safe, but birds were
dying. Her friend asked Carson to look into the matter.

Carson did, and the more she learned, she said, "the more appalled
I became." Some of her findings weren't new. Back in 1952, Dwight D.
Eisenhower had been elected president on a pro-business platform. The US Fish
and Wildlife Service was then the only government agency with a mandate
to protect nature. Eisenhower dismissed the conservationist who headed the
agency, replacing him with a political pawn who had no intention of protecting
the environment if that conflicted with business interests.

The development of pesticides had been important to the war effort
during World War II. Soldiers on tropical fronts had to be protected from
disease-carrying insects. In 1939, a scientist had discovered that a substance
called DDT was very effective in killing these pests. When DDT was used to
kill the disease-carrying insects threatening US troops, it seemed to be a
miracle substance, able to kill hundreds of species at once. Its inventor was

awarded the Nobel Prize, and the potent pesticide was sometimes credited with winning the war.

After the war, DDT was marketed to farmers and homeowners. Farmers used decommissioned fighter planes to dust crops with it, and housewives squirted it from spray "guns." There were almost no objections to the wide use of the powerful pesticide.

writing her masterpiece

Carson spent four years researching the destructive effect of DDT and other pesticides on ecosystems and humans and the way the chemical industry tried to mislead the public about those effects. She knew it would not be easy to persuade people that disrupting nature through technology was disastrous. Carson began by writing a letter to the *Washington Post*. "The real wealth of the nation," she said, "lies in the resources of the earth—soil, water, forests, minerals, and wildlife." She declared that finding a balance between using those resources for current needs and preserving them for the future could not be a political issue. As she wrote: "It is one of the ironies of our time that, while concentrating on the defense of our country against enemies from without, we should be so heedless of those who would destroy it from within."

Carson learned that DDT was a carcinogen—a cancer-causing substance. After it entered the food chain, it exposed the entire ecosystem to harm. She began to see the power of the manufacturers of pesticides when the US Supreme Court refused to stop gypsy moth–spraying on Long Island after the spray was shown to cause cancer. But the case got the public's attention.

ecosystems

An ecosystem is made up of all the interacting plants and animals that share an environment, along with the nonliving things that help the living ones survive, such as sunlight and water. The "system" in ecosystem describes the way these species and elements depend on one another. If one part of the ecosystem is harmed, the rest of the system is affected. Rachel Carson discovered that when DDT killed insects, it also killed other parts of the insects' ecosystem, such as the birds that eat them—and it polluted the environment, including crops eaten by humans. Through her research for her book *Silent Spring*, she learned the disastrous effect of targeting one part of an ecosystem with a poisonous substance.

The stress of the work took a terrible toll on Carson's health, causing ulcers and exhaustion. But only when she was diagnosed with breast cancer did she have to pause. The doctor performed surgery in 1960 but gave her no further treatments. He did not tell her she had a malignant tumor, and the cancer spread through her body as she went on writing.

Silent Spring was serialized in the *New Yorker* in three parts. On June 16, 1962, the first part prompted more letters from readers than anything the magazine had ever published. The most haunting passage was a fable about a US town that experienced "a spring without voices." Adults and children were dying unexpectedly. Where once a chorus of birdsong had filled the mornings, now "only silence lay over the fields and woods and marshes." On the farms, Carson wrote, "hens brooded, but no chicks hatched." And "the people had done it themselves."

Silent Spring, published in September 1962, became an instant best seller and was called the most controversial book of the year.

the opposition fires back

In one way, the American public was ready to listen to Carson's warnings about the dangers of pesticide. They had seen other examples of substances that had harmed humans. For instance, in the mid-1950s, testing of atom bombs had left residues of a radioactive substance in cow's milk. Parents were outraged that children were drinking such poison. Then, in the early 1960s, women in Europe who had taken the medication thalidomide had babies born with severe birth defects. All these developments raised people's consciousness of new threats in modern life. Science did not always bring progress.

But Carson's ideas faced fierce opposition. The chemical industry launched a counterattack, accusing her of wanting to return to the Dark Ages and suggesting she had lost her mind. But everything she cited was backed by expert research. John F. Kennedy, the new president, ordered a science advisory committee to examine the issues, and the committee confirmed her claims.

For the first time, the public was alarmed by the prospect of damage to human genes caused by exposure to pesticides. Such damage could lead to cancer—along with pollution and the extinction of whole species. Still, ignorance abounded everywhere. A former US secretary of agriculture asked, "Why is a spinster with no children so concerned about genetics?" Such a remark was meant to dismiss her (and women in general).

Terminal cancer landed Carson back in the hospital often. But she gave speeches, appeared on television, and testified before Congress. After having composed so many lyrically beautiful descriptions of a nature that was eternal, she spent the little time left to her on Earth to make sure people understood that nature was, after all, vulnerable. Humans could easily destroy it.

Carson died on April 14, 1964. She had seen people wake up to the danger that so anguished her. She had mostly beaten the special interests that tried to discredit her.

Her work also contributed to a powerful change at the highest levels of government. Spurred by her work, the federal government realized it needed to take action against pollution.

The 1970 passage of a National Environmental Policy Act set the stage for the formation of a government agency devoted solely to protecting natural resources. On April 22, 1970, twenty million Americans celebrated the first Earth Day to show their support for this goal.

Other agencies already monitored air pollution and food and water safety. On July 9, 1970, President Richard Nixon sent a plan to Congress for a new, independent agency to take over these jobs. The US Environmental Protection Agency (EPA) opened in December 1970 with the goal of treating all forms of pollution as a single problem that the new agency would fight.

The *EPA Journal* has stated, "EPA today may be said without exaggeration to be the extended shadow of Rachel Carson." Carson didn't live to see its founding. But she must have felt that her life had been well spent. *Silent Spring* is one of the few books that changed the course of history.

*"The history of life on earth
is the history of the interaction of
living things and their surroundings."*

—rachel carson, *silent spring*

GERTRUDE BERG

writer, producer, star

1899–1966

Gertrude Berg was the sole creator and star performer of one of the first sitcoms. From 1929 on, when the brand-new radio networks reached out to every corner of the nation, people on farms, in towns, and in cities gathered around their radio sets to listen to an immigrant Jewish family cope with life in New York. They made The Rise of the Goldbergs among the most popular shows on the air. Before the internet or even television, radio was the medium that united Americans during the Great Depression and made Gertrude Berg the first woman media powerhouse. Her affectionate portrait of immigrants struggling to adapt amused, comforted, and enlightened listeners for nearly forty years.

gertrude berg was born Tillie Edelstein on October 3, 1899, in

East Harlem, New York. Tillie's father was a large-hearted, rather moody man who ran a restaurant. Her mother was eager to become a "real" American and rejected many of the Jewish traditions observed by her own parents. Tillie's maternal grandparents lived around the corner. Before leaving for school, Tillie would lean out her window and call, "Yoo-hoo, Grandma, what time is it?"

She was just as fond of her grandfather, Mordecai. His devotion to democracy and the American Dream helped to shape Tillie's own liberal beliefs. She dreamed, she said, of "doing something on my own." Once, walking with him, she pointed to a theater marquee and said, "See that, Grandpa? My name is going to be there some day." "It is your America," he would tell her, meaning she had a right—and the opportunity—to succeed. Tillie would use the quirky, colorful characters in her family to make her mark.

turning life into stories

The many little apartments in the Edelsteins' building centered around a dumbwaiter, which was like a small elevator used to carry goods. Its shaft opened into all the homes, so the neighbors' troubles and triumphs could be overheard by everyone else. If there was a problem, someone always knew exactly what the solution was and didn't hesitate to recommend it by shouting into the dumbwaiter shaft. Tillie learned a lot about life. It was raw material for her imagination.

When Tillie was seven, her father bought a rundown estate in the Catskill region of New York State and turned it into a hotel for vacationing Jewish families. Tillie was supposed to keep the children amused on rainy days. She made up skits and plays, and before long she was performing them for the adults as well.

There was sadness in her life, but no one talked about it. Her brother died young and her mother's grief led first to a breakdown and finally to placement in an institution. That left a mark on Tillie. The characters she later created would be multifaceted people who reflected the range of life's experiences, not caricatures.

becoming gertrude berg

Lewis Berg, an engineering student from England, arrived at the hotel for the summer of 1910 and was struck by Tillie, young as she was. They married in 1918, when Tillie was nineteen. Lewis took a job at a sugar plantation in Louisiana. Yanked from the only world she knew, Berg was miserable. She consoled herself by writing plays based on her family. She and Lewis had two children, and she added them to the scripts as the children of her leading character, Molly Goldberg, and Molly's husband, Jake.

When the plantation where Lewis worked burned down, the Bergs moved back to New York. Tillie Berg established a disciplined, even compulsive routine that revolved around her work. She had a goal. Radio was becoming a force in American life, and she wanted to be in on it. She hoped to sell a script called *The Rise of the Goldbergs* (the "rise of" in the title was a tribute to the idea of opportunity) to one of the networks. Because it sounded more dignified, Tillie changed her name to Gertrude.

the goldbergs

Jewish comedians had long been a staple of stereotypical humor in vaudeville. Berg offered *The Rise of the Goldbergs* as the antidote: The Goldberg family, based on real people, was portrayed with affection and respect.

She gave the executives at NBC a handwritten script, gambling that they couldn't read her writing and would ask her to perform it. They did, and she was so good she was hired to play the main part as well as write the scripts. Berg was responsible for writing, casting, producing, directing, and performing in a show that ran for fifteen minutes six nights a week. She even paid the actors from her own wages, which were seventy-five dollars a week. Berg was on her way to becoming the first woman media powerhouse.

The Rise of the Goldbergs premiered on November 29, 1929—one month after the stock market crash that began the Great Depression. Audiences experiencing the economic troubles of the Depression needed distraction and comfort. They quickly identified with the Goldbergs and their challenges. After three weeks, Gertrude lost her voice and a substitute went on the air in her place. NBC received 115,000 letters demanding to know what had happened to her. Molly's call of "Yoo-hoo! Mrs. Bloom," which she yelled from her window, was becoming a national catchphrase. She based the idea on her childhood memories of her grandmother.

early radio

While ordinary citizens experimented with radio broadcasts as early as 1906, radio was mostly used only by the US military. The first broadcast meant for the public came in 1920.

Radio caught on quickly. Families sat around their sets at night to listen to their favorite shows together. Shows included news programs, plays, mystery series, quiz shows, children's shows, concerts, and situation comedies like *The Rise of the Goldbergs*.

The show's humor came from the characters and the way they talked. *The Goldbergs'* intonation and word order showed that her family had once spoken another language, Yiddish. Molly Goldberg showered her family with love, meddled in everyone's business, and often dispensed practical solutions to their problems, just as the neighbors had via the dumbwaiter of her childhood.

The Goldbergs, like everyone else in the country, were striving to get along with others and to better their lot. The audience could identify, whether they had been in America for centuries or were recent arrivals from Eastern Europe, Ireland, or Italy. Listening to the show was especially poignant for Jewish families, for their culture was being celebrated, not stereotyped.

success on the radio

The show's name was shortened, becoming simply *The Goldbergs* in 1936. As the years went on, Gertrude and her husband grew rich, living on upscale Park Avenue in New York City. Still, she went back regularly to Jewish immigrant neighborhoods to listen to people talk. Authenticity was important to her. Even the sound effects on the show were authentic. If the script called for frying an egg, one was actually fried in the studio. When a character washed her hair, the actor lathered her own hair with real shampoo. When the Goldberg family's son was drafted during World War II, the show was broadcast from Grand Central Station, where the family said good-bye to him before he boarded a train.

The Goldbergs was an invitation to Americans to continue believing in the good life despite the Great Depression, and they responded with devotion. According to polls at the time, Berg was the most admired woman in the United States after Eleanor Roosevelt, the First Lady. Asked why the show was so popular, Gertrude said that ethnic groups were only different on the surface and "these surface differences serve to emphasize how much alike most people are underneath."

As Americans moved to the suburbs after World War II ended in 1945, so did the Goldbergs. And as more and more families had a television set, radio lost its appeal. Gertrude, who never let an opportunity pass, prepared to go before the cameras.

television and the black list

The Goldbergs debuted on CBS television in 1949 and soon had an audience of forty million. Not only was the show hugely popular, but it won awards for excellence. Gertrude was conquering the new medium, just as she had done with radio.

Television was supposed to bring families back together, after the war and new freedoms for young people had separated them. *The Goldbergs* was about family life and also neighborliness, so it was perfect for the new form of entertainment. The theme of pride in America was also strong on the show, with portraits of Washington and Lincoln prominently displayed in the Goldberg household. Ironically, the Jewish show paved the way for the "white bread" family sitcoms of the 1950s and '60s.

"white bread" family sitcoms

In the earliest days of television there were three major networks: ABC, CBS, and NBC. Network executives focused on developing prime-time shows that a family might watch together, like pioneers gathered around a hearth. At first the shows featured some working-class families and diversity.

But as production of the shows moved to Hollywood in the middle of the 1950s, the shows became less diverse. By 1960 "white bread" situation comedies were typical. These sitcoms were about privileged, white middle-class suburban families like those of *Leave It to Beaver* and *Father Knows Best*. They have been nicknamed for bland, flavorless white bread.

The 1950s had a dark undercurrent of fear that was especially damaging to people in the entertainment industry. The nation was undergoing a Red Scare—a fear of Communists in government and cultural institutions.

the red scare

The Red Scare began in 1950 when Senator Joseph McCarthy claimed that hundreds of people who worked for the US government were Communists—people who believed in a system of government where people share all property and goods. But such an arrangement was a threat to a capitalist system. Furthermore, the Soviet Union was Communist and America's enemy during the 1950s. A committee called the House Un-American Activities Committee, or HUAC, already existed to investigate possible Communists, who were considered enemies of the government. Fueled by the hysteria of the Red Scare, HUAC led investigations that forced people to testify and to "name names" of anyone they knew to be Communists.

In June 1950, a right-wing journal published a pamphlet called *Red Channels* listing people in show business who were suspected of Communist activity or leanings. This became an industry "blacklist." To protect their products from being associated with Communist-leaning talent, sponsors of radio and television programs ordered producers to fire anyone on the list. Philip Loeb, who played Molly's husband, Jake, on *The Goldbergs*, was on it.

Gertrude refused to fire Loeb. She believed he was not a Communist, and in any case, she, like many people in the entertainment industry, hated the idea of a blacklist. But her advertising sponsor lacked her courage, and CBS canceled the show. Berg then tried to sell it to another sponsor, with Loeb still playing her husband, and got nowhere. Finally she told him, with deep regret, that she had to let him go. He was replaced.

When Loeb couldn't find work anywhere else, she paid his salary herself. A few years later, Philip Loeb committed suicide. His death haunted Berg for the rest of her life.

Although Berg herself was accused of sympathizing with Communism, she eventually won a new contract with NBC. But she had been off the air for months, and television had moved on without her. Now most shows were "father-centered." Strong mothers and ethnic characters were out. (The exception was *I Love Lucy*, which featured a Cuban husband. It took over the old *Goldbergs* time slot at CBS.)

act three

Gertrude Berg had stressed the similarities between herself and Molly Goldberg for so long, many people thought she didn't have to do much acting to make the character believable. So could she act? Could she play a different person? The answer came when she was cast in several television dramas, to great acclaim. But her heart was always with *The Goldbergs*. She fought for and won a contract with the DuMont Television Network, and when the program lost money, she signed with a company that would film episodes of the show instead of broadcasting it live.

The executives demanded that the Goldberg family be "modernized," meaning made less ethnic. Berg had no choice in the matter. The show died a gradual death, even as she reinvented herself as a theater actress.

Work was everything to her. Refusing to be defeated, Berg toured in summer stock theater, staying in grungy hotel rooms and playing in dilapidated theaters.

She triumphed in several popular plays and returned to television for one more season, in a show about a middle-aged woman who attends college. She worked and worked and worked, right up until the day before she died of heart failure in September 1966.

Gertrude Berg's greatest contribution to American culture was through radio. She used it to educate as well as to entertain. A very particular family touched a mass audience through their common humanity.

"And when I am by myself
sometimes I wonder—
did I really become the
woman I wanted to be—
or am I still trying?"

—gertrude berg

SHIRLEY CHISHOLM

political trailblazer

1924–2005

Barack Obama was the first Black president, and Hillary Clinton was the first woman to become the presidential nominee of a major political party—but a generation before them, there was Shirley Chisholm. In 1968, she was the first African American woman elected to Congress. Only four years later, she boldly campaigned for the Democratic nomination for president, the first Black woman to do so. She wanted to be a catalyst for change and to represent all the people who had been overlooked by political leaders. She paved the way for every woman candidate since and is an inspiration to all who care about social progress.

shirley st. hill was born in Brooklyn, New York, on November 30, 1924. Her parents had come to the United States from Barbados, a Caribbean island whose people had been migrating to Brooklyn for over a century.

a fierce little girl

Shirley was a straight-backed, keenly intelligent child with a lot of style. It was clear from the age of two, her mother said, that she would achieve important things.

But her parents struggled to raise their family on very limited earnings. Because living was cheaper in Barbados, they sent their three daughters to a grandmother's farm there.

Under her grandmother's loving care in Barbados, Shirley's self-confidence grew. "I learned from an early age I was somebody," she later said. "I didn't need the Black revolution to teach me that."

When Shirley was ten, the family was reunited in Brooklyn. It was a shock to move from balmy, nurturing Barbados to cold, teeming, noisy Brooklyn. Worse, because she hadn't studied US history, she was put in the third grade instead of the sixth, where she belonged. She rebelled over that injustice by snapping rubber bands at others and shooting spitballs. Finally, her teacher arranged for tutoring so she could catch up, and she was put in her rightful grade.

enduring segregation

Her parents moved the family to Brooklyn's Bedford-Stuyvesant neighborhood, where Shirley encountered open racial bias for the first time. There was even a chapter of the Ku Klux Klan.

the ku klux klan

The Ku Klux Klan, formed just months after the Civil War ended, violently attacked the newly freed slaves and anyone who supported their rights. Often working in the secrecy of nighttime, the Klan burned crosses, churches, and houses and beat and killed innocent people. In the 1960s, in response to the Civil Rights Movement, they again targeted Black Americans. The Klan still exists today with an estimated five thousand to eight thousand members.

Shirley's mother made sure the children worked hard in school and visited the library every week. Shirley was determined to rise in the world, to make something of herself—and to help others. Her father taught her that political activism could improve the lives of poor people.

Shirley was admitted to the elite Girls' High School, whose students came from all over Brooklyn—half of them Black. She was a star student. At graduation she was offered scholarships to two excellent colleges, Vassar and Oberlin, but the family could not afford to pay for her room and board, so, reluctantly, she applied to Brooklyn College.

Brooklyn College set her life's course.

finding a future in college

Brooklyn College had sixty Black students out of a total of a thousand. Being in the minority only made Shirley more determined. She studied hard and excelled.

She joined the Harriet Tubman Society, where current issues and problems were discussed. Through the Debating Society, she became an effective public speaker. A white professor told her she ought to go into politics. At first she thought that was an impossible idea, since she was Black and a woman. But her fellow students encouraged her, too.

Shirley became a teacher. In 1939, she married an admiring young man named Conrad Chisholm. After earning a master's degree in early childhood education from Columbia University, she ran a nursery school and a day care center. But her mind was already on politics. Brooklyn had the biggest Democratic "machine" in the country. The Democratic Party there was run by longtime "bosses" who made all the decisions for the group.

entering politics at ground level

Shirley Chisholm joined the Bedford-Stuyvesant Democratic Club, but its meetings were segregated by race. Moreover, the club didn't nominate Black candidates to represent the Black voters who lived in the district. The club also discriminated by sex: women were not allowed to attend meetings, although they did most of the fund-raising and behind-the-scenes work for the club. Chisholm organized them to demand the right to attend meetings and have their voices heard. This earned the men's grudging respect.

Chisholm rose in the ranks of the Democratic Party, speaking at rallies and confronting City Hall about issues like making sure trash was collected and police patrolled the streets.

Next, she actively campaigned for a Black candidate in a primary election, ringing doorbells and organizing workers. The candidate's victory forced the established party—the machine—to pay attention to Black voters. By 1960, the peaceful sit-ins by young Black civil rights activists at segregated

SHIRLEY CHISHOLM for PRESIDENT

UNBOUGHT 19 72 UNBOSSED

Woolworth's lunch counters— where Blacks weren't served—in the South alerted the nation to the growing battle for equal rights for Black people. Brooklyn Blacks saw a chance for real change.

Leaders of the Black Power Movement began demanding better living conditions in Brooklyn. They favored a separate Black community, but Chisholm believed in integration. She was also excited by the women's movement, which was trying to change laws to give women equal opportunities in education, the workplace, and other areas. She decided to concentrate her efforts on reforming the Democratic Party, which was not keeping pace with these movements.

Shirley Chisholm ran for the state legislature in 1965. It was a job she thought she had earned as a party worker. She had done so much canvassing— going door to door to get support for candidates and issues—that she knew her district well. The Democratic Party bosses opposed her because she was such an outspoken woman, but there were more female voters than male ones, and women backed her enthusiastically. In the middle of her campaign, her father suddenly died. It was a horrible loss for Shirley, who adored him, but she went on campaigning and easily defeated her opponents.

loneliness of the state legislator

Chisholm served four years in Albany, the New York State capital. She suffered discrimination there, mostly because she was a woman. None of the other legislators invited her to have dinner, and she couldn't dine unaccompanied as an African American woman. She spent her evenings alone in her hotel room. This was hard for her, for she loved to dance and dress in elegant fashions. But she was an effective legislator who stuck to her ideals.

Hers was the first bill to grant unemployment benefits to domestic workers—maids, nannies, and health aides—in New York State. The president, Lyndon B. Johnson, had a progressive agenda called the Great Society, which aimed to eliminate social ills such as poverty and discrimination while improving education, health care, and the environment, among other goals. In harmony with Johnson's program, Chisholm fought for access to education and day care for African Americans, Latinxs, and immigrants. When her Brooklyn leadership expected her to vote for their candidate for House Speaker, she defied them and voted for the other guy. All this made her a force to be reckoned with. Her contrary stand was popular with voters.

unbought and unbossed

She decided to run for the US House of Representatives in 1968, with a slogan that reflected her actions in Albany: "Unbought and Unbossed." She would do what was right, not what the party, or anyone else, told her to do. America was bitterly divided between those who resisted change and those who embraced it, including Vietnam War opponents and women's and civil rights activists.

The congressional district that Chisholm wanted to represent had been made up of parts of many different Brooklyn neighborhoods. In 1967, the lines of Brooklyn's congressional districts were redrawn. Now the majority of voters in the district were African American. For the first time, Black voters had the numbers to elect someone who actually represented them. The 1968 election would be unusually historic.

The nation reeled that year when Martin Luther King Jr. and Robert Kennedy were assassinated. Chisholm grieved over their deaths, but she pressed on with her campaign.

She and her opponent, James Farmer, the head of the Congress for Racial Equality (CORE), actually agreed on most of the issues. But he didn't live in Brooklyn, she complained, and he was sexist. His flyers said he presented a "strong male image" and would provide a "man's voice" in Washington, DC. Even the media coverage was sexist; TV and radio ignored her entirely. But when the tiny Chisholm debated the burly Farmer, she became a giant. Her skills as a thinker and speaker, her belief in herself and in her mission to help others, all propelled her to victory.

in the nation's capital

Chisholm's election as the first Black woman representative to Congress in November 1968 made her a national figure overnight. She entered the House of Representatives on a mission to end poverty, provide services to minorities, and reform Congress itself. It operated on a "seniority" system, giving more power to the members who had been there the longest. She called it the "senility system."

The House gave her a hostile reception. As the only Black woman, Chisholm endured insults and scorn with dignity and a sense of humor. One southern congressman spat into his handkerchief whenever she passed him. No one would sit with her in the cafeteria. When President Nixon's administration increased defense spending for weapons, cutting the budget for a preschool program called Head Start, Chisholm was incensed. She took the floor and delivered a powerful anti-war speech, promising to vote against every military appropriation bill. As she walked back to her seat, she heard one representative mutter to another, "You know, she is crazy."

Crazy, no. Committed, yes: She was pro-education, anti-war, and the strongest feminist in Congress. In 1970, she reintroduced the Equal Rights Amendment for national gender equality, originally offered in 1923 by a suffragist named Alice Paul. When Chisholm reintroduced the amendment, she said she supported it because she had faced even more prejudice as a woman than as a Black person. In fact, in 1970, she published a magazine article titled "I'd Rather be Black than Female."

Chisholm helped found the Congressional Black Caucus, then made up of a handful of people. She was the leader of the crusade for the rights of women, immigrants, domestic workers, and even for gay rights, way ahead of her time. She was a ferocious champion of the underdog.

In 1970, Chisholm joined Gloria Steinem, Bella Abzug, and Betty Friedan, all major figures in the women's movement, to found the National Women's Political Caucus, dedicated to increasing *women's* participation in the *political* process. Chisholm worked to broaden the predominantly white movement, encouraging more women of color to join. Courageously at the time, she announced her support for reproductive choice. "To label family planning and legal abortion *genocide* is male rhetoric for male ears," she said. Chisholm always spoke her mind and voted her conscience, and it made her popular. In 1970, she was reelected with 80 percent of the vote.

a trailblazing candidacy

The civil rights struggle, the anti-war movement, and women's liberation were multigenerational, but the majority of those who marched and protested for these causes were young people. Chisholm wanted to carry their causes forward, and in 1972, the National Feminist Party nominated her for president of the United States. While she always did have some key male mentors and champions, the male leaders of various Black civil rights organizations opposed her candidacy. These leaders felt that they had more of an advantage by endorsing a major white candidate than by supporting Shirley Chisholm. Chisholm said she never expected them to support her. She told a gathering of Black women she was running because she was tired of "tokenism and look-how-far-we have-comeism."

Although Chisholm campaigned in several states, she didn't expect to win, only to inspire others to break barriers. She wanted to shake up the system and shine a light on marginalized people. Throughout, she was denounced as arrogant and told she didn't know her place. A news article falsely claimed she was in a mental institution. Three times, while campaigning along what was called the "Chisholm Trail," someone attacked her, one man with a knife. After the election, Chisholm returned to Congress, reelected with 87 percent of the vote. She tried to save what was left of President Johnson's progressive Great Society program after President Nixon took office and in the years following. But politics and government became much more conservative. Chisholm realized, especially after the election of President Ronald Reagan, that she could no longer serve her constituents. She stepped down in 1983.

After her seven terms in Congress, Chisholm taught politics and sociology at Mount Holyoke College and went on giving fiery speeches, visiting 150 college campuses. She died in Florida on New Year's Day, 2005.

Shirley Chisholm was a born politician with high ideals and deeply practical instincts. She learned to play a man's game, and she earned the trust of those with whom she had to work. She was able to laugh at the absurdity of the gross prejudice she encountered in her public career. She had courage and grace.

In 2015, President Obama awarded her a posthumous Presidential Medal of Freedom, America's highest civilian honor. He said of her, "There are people in our country's history who don't look left or right—they just look straight ahead. Shirley Chisholm was one of those people."

"From the time I was two, my mother said I was born to lead."

—shirley chisholm

PATSY MINK

champion for women and girls in education

1927–2002

Patsy Mink opened the doors to equal opportunity in education and beyond for girls and women. Her insistence on justice and fairness stemmed from her own early experience of prejudice as a Japanese American and a woman. That very personal crusade was inspired by decades of discrimination against all women and minorities. Mink sponsored legislation that began righting those long-standing wrongs. She endured defeats as well as victories but never let up her fierce pressure on indifferent authorities. As a member of Congress, she was the coauthor and driving force behind the law mandating equality in education for women and girls: Title IX of the Education Amendments of 1972. The law led to a surge of female athletes, as well as women in fields such as STEM (science, technology, engineering, and math), law, and medicine. She was a true public servant who wrote progressive bills that would help people—and she got them passed. Her life demonstrates the power of good government.

patsy takemoto was born on December 6, 1927, in Paia, on the island of Maui in what was then Hawaii Territory (not yet a state). Her grandparents had emigrated from Japan, and her parents were born in Hawaii. But after Japan attacked Pearl Harbor in 1941, all Japanese Americans were suspected of disloyalty—sometimes by their neighbors, other times even by the government. One night, her father, a civil engineer who had served in the US Army for a year, was taken away for interrogation, simply because of his Japanese ancestry. When he came home, he burned all his Japanese keepsakes. Nevertheless, the family didn't feel safe until the war ended. "It made me realize that one could not take citizenship and the promise of the US Constitution for granted," Mink later wrote.

a legacy of discrimination

Patsy's Japanese ancestors had come to Hawaii to work on sugar plantations. When she was growing up, Hawaiian society was organized plantation-style, with white bosses and workers of color. The workers struggled against racial discrimination, including low pay and poor conditions. Those who were lucky enough to become students often had to drop out to help support their families. Patsy began defying that norm right away. She was a star student with abundant energy and charm, so popular with her fellow students, she was elected president of her high school senior class. In those days, girls were almost never elected to anything but secretary. She was also valedictorian, the top honor for a high school graduate. She wanted to be a doctor.

She started college at age sixteen at the University of Hawaii, then applied to several medical schools and was rejected by all of them, some stating openly that they turned her down because she was a woman. She hadn't expected that. "It was the most devastating disappointment in my life," she said. She was thrown off course for a short while. Then a mentor told Patsy the world wasn't closed; she should apply to other graduate schools. Patsy decided to study law. At that moment, the crusader for equality was born.

She was one of two women accepted to her class at the University of Chicago Law School. (The university probably admitted her because it thought she was a foreign student, she later said.) But she couldn't pay the tuition. After searching, she found a scholarship for children of veterans and applied. She won it. That was a turning point that opened a great new adventure.

She met John Mink, a graduate student in geology, who was attracted to her remarkable charisma. "People just looked at her and wanted to be with her," he wrote. They married on January 27, 1951, and after Patsy Mink graduated that year she began looking for a job. But again she found all doors closed to her as a woman and as a person of Japanese descent. In 1952, she had a child, a daughter named Gwendolyn.

The Minks moved to Honolulu, hoping Patsy would have better luck, but she didn't. Potential employers turned her away on the grounds that her priority should be serving her husband. With no offers, she opened her own law office and taught classes at the university.

Having grown up glued to the radio during President Franklin D. Roosevelt's Fireside Chats to the nation, she believed government could change people's lives for the better. She decided to enter politics. Hawaii strongly leaned Republican, which meant serving the interests of the plantation owners. Mink was a Democrat, as FDR had been. To bring other energetic young people into the party, she founded the Oahu Young Democrats. In 1955, she ran for the territorial house of representatives and was elected, then reelected. She was the first Japanese American woman to serve there. She went on to win two terms in the Hawaii senate. At the time, the government was testing nuclear weapons in the Pacific, and the fallout threatened Hawaii. Mink fought to ban the testing and was vilified by anti-Communists who thought it was necessary to keep the Soviet Union at bay. Mink was establishing herself as a fierce advocate for her views, no matter whom they might offend.

an upstart campaign

When Hawaii became a state in 1959, Mink ran for its seat in the US House of Representatives. She lost but was invited to speak at the national Democratic convention in 1960, where she delivered a rousing call for a strong civil rights platform. In 1964, she again ran for a seat in the US House, without the endorsement of the party bosses. This meant she had to run and finance her own campaign. Her husband, John, was her campaign manager, all the workers were volunteers, and the budget was tiny. But she reached voters, who liked her. Mink won the election, becoming the first Asian American woman and the first woman of color in Congress.

Mink was too independent minded for the Democratic bosses in Hawaii, who tried repeatedly to oust her by running primary opponents against her. But the people were on her side and she won five terms in the House.

After President John F. Kennedy was assassinated in 1963, President Lyndon B. Johnson launched an ambitious program called the Great Society, intended to lift up America's downtrodden. Patsy Mink was its vigorous supporter. She worked hard for education and economic equality. She sponsored or introduced bills helping families pay for childcare and student loans, and she helped launch Head Start, which provides preschool services for lower-income families.

During Johnson's presidency, the United States was sending troops to Vietnam. Like many people, Mink was morally outraged by the war there. Because Hawaii's economy depended on its military bases, her opposition to the war made her more enemies at home.

smashing the barriers

As an outspoken woman, Mink had to avoid any signs of emotional weakness, or men wouldn't take her seriously. But she was passionate and earned a reputation for self-righteousness, which didn't sit well with many men. Mink joined with the ten other women in Congress to promote legislation to end gender discrimination. They took direct action, too, storming the all-male congressional gym and winning the right to use it.

In 1972 she entered the presidential primary in Oregon on an anti-war platform. The result was a resounding defeat. But that year, Mink made her most important contribution to history. Along with Representative Edith Green of Oregon and Senator Birch Bayh of Indiana, she wrote Title IX, considered the most important of the amendments in the Education Amendments of 1972 bill. Title IX required coeducational institutions receiving federal funds to offer equal opportunities to girls. At that time, women were less than 10 percent of law and medical school students.

Title IX was signed into law in 1972. Now admissions officers had to consider women's applications the same way they did those of men. Equipment and participation in sports programs had to be proportional to the percentage of girls enrolled.

five payoffs of title ix of the education amendments of 1972

1. **Equal access to higher education:** Before Title IX, colleges and universities could legally refuse to admit women—and some did. Now colleges can't discriminate against applicants on the basis of their gender.

2. **Career education:** Before Title IX, many high schools didn't allow girls to take traditionally "male" classes, such as shop and auto mechanics. Nor could boys take home economics, which focused on housekeeping skills, such as cooking. Now schools have to let students choose their own career-preparation classes, regardless of gender.

3. **Employment:** Before Title IX, schools could discriminate against women when making hiring decisions. For instance, they could fire a woman teacher who became pregnant. Under Title IX, such discrimination is illegal.

4. **Fighting sexual harassment:** School administrators used to be able to overlook claims of sexual harassment. Under Title IX, schools must both try to prevent sexual harassment, and address all reports of it.

5. **Access to athletics:** Equal access to sports is the most widely known impact of Title IX. Before Title IX, one in twenty-seven girls played varsity high school sports. Today, two in five play, and they can get athletic scholarships because college sports for women are popular and widely available.

Until the passage of Title IX, varsity sports for girls in public schools and universities didn't receive the same funding, level of participation, or crowds as men's sports. Suddenly, equipment, supplies, playing fields, gyms, and locker rooms all had to be of equal quality. Girls who had never had a chance to develop athletic skills were playing on teams, becoming healthier, stronger, more confident, and more competitive, and developing leadership qualities in other areas of their lives as well.

Having been used to receiving more than 99 percent of athletic budgets, coaches in men's sports fought back, lobbying Congress to pass amendments exempting popular men's sports from the Act. After intense debate, an amendment to exempt moneymaking men's sports from Title IX came to a vote in the House of Representatives. It was rejected, but Mink still had to fight to make sure Title IX included athletics.

It was up to the US Department of Health, Education, and Welfare to put Title IX into action. Members of Congress who thought it would hurt men's college sports forced a new vote to exempt certain moneymaking sports.

Patsy Mink was in the cloakroom, waiting to cast her vote, when she received a phone call. Her daughter, Gwendolyn, had been in a terrible automobile accident. Her colleagues told her she must go to her daughter. Mink left, and the veto overturning the rule applying Title IX to all sports won by a single vote. Title IX for equality in athletics was doomed.

title ix: the law

"No person in the United States shall, on the basis of sex, be excluded from participation in, be denied the benefits of, or be subjected to discrimination under any education program or activity receiving Federal financial assistance." —Title IX, signed into law on June 23, 1972

But when Mink returned to Washington, the Speaker of the House called for a new vote. This time Title IX was saved. A new world had been opened to girls and women. Women's sports would be transformed, and so would the professional world. Two years later, Mink introduced the Women's Education Equity Act, which provided thirty million dollars a year to help poor women attend schools and to remove gender stereotypes in textbooks. The law passed.

Mink was a shoo-in to be reelected to the House that year, but she took a big gamble and gave up that scat to run for the Senate. Once again, she did it without the support of the party bosses. This time, she didn't succeed. Ousted from Washington, she ran for governor of Hawaii and lost, then ran for mayor of Honolulu and lost again.

She remained in public service. During the administration of President Jimmy Carter, she served as an assistant secretary of state.

Mink was reelected to Congress in 1990, but the mood of the country had changed. Former president Ronald Reagan had denied that government was the solution to anything—rather, he labeled it the problem. Federal programs designed to help people were under attack. Nevertheless, Mink pushed for a universal health care plan. But she had to devote most of her energy to resisting efforts to reduce already-existing government programs.

In 2002, she was expected to win reelection when she caught chicken pox, which led to pneumonia. She died on September 28, 2002. In her honor, Title IX was renamed the Patsy T. Mink Equal Opportunity in Education Act. Patsy Mink's great legacy for generations of American women is nothing less than the opportunity to pursue their dreams.

"*If to believe in freedom and equality is to be a radical, then I am a radical. So long as there remain groups of our fellow Americans who are denied equal opportunity and equal protection under the law . . . we must remain steadfast, till all shades of man may stand side by side in dignity and self-respect to truly enjoy the fruits of this great land.*"

—patsy mink

VERA RUBIN

queen of dark matter

1928–2016

Astronomer Vera Rubin made one of the twentieth century's most unexpected and important discoveries about our universe. Astronomy was the study of light that reaches Earth from the visible heavens. Rubin boldly chose to look at the areas of the universe that don't emit light. Her research confirmed the existence of dark matter—an invisible form of matter that has a gravitational pull. She transformed our understanding of what the cosmos is made of and how vast it is. She encouraged younger women to become scientists, serving as a living model for how to open up a field that was a virtual men's club. Her intellect, curiosity, and persistence overcame countless obstacles. Vera Rubin was always most excited by the unknown. She was a true visionary, yet she never sought the spotlight. Fittingly, she chose as her subject the 84 percent of the universe that is invisible.

The astronomer who unlocked the vast spaces between the stars was born **vera florence cooper** in Philadelphia on July 23, 1928. Both her parents had emigrated from Eastern Europe and were engineers at Bell Labs, the technology research arm of Bell Telephone. Vera's earliest memories were of lying in bed near a window, entranced by the night sky. "There was just nothing as interesting in my life as watching the stars every night," she said. "I found it a remarkable thing. You could tell time by the stars. I could see meteors."

A children's book about Maria Mitchell, the nineteenth-century astronomer who taught at Vassar College, inspired Vera to learn more about the stars. Mitchell, encouraged at a young age by her father to pursue her interest in the heavens, became the first professional female astronomer in the United States.

By the time Vera was twelve, she could memorize the paths of meteors she saw in the night sky and map them in the morning. Her father helped her build a cardboard telescope and drove her to meetings of amateur astronomers.

diving into galaxies

A high school teacher warned her to steer clear of science, because as a girl, she would only be frustrated. But Vera had set her heart on astronomy. Because of Maria Mitchell, she never thought she *couldn't* be an astronomer. Mitchell had taught at Vassar, so Vera applied there and won a full scholarship. She majored in astronomy—the only student in the class of 1948 to do so.

She needed to go to graduate school to become a scientist. Her first choice was Princeton, which, she soon learned, didn't admit women. She then applied to Harvard and was accepted but had to withdraw because she was marrying Robert Rubin, a young mathematician and physicist, and would follow him to Cornell. (The director of the Harvard Observatory scrawled on his letter to her, "Damn you women! Every time I get a good one ready, she goes off and gets married.")

Cornell didn't have a great astronomy department, but its physics department was star-studded: Hans Bethe, a pioneer in quantum physics; Richard Feynman, who would win the Nobel Prize in Physics in 1965 and became her thesis advisor; Martha Carpenter, who had a passion for galaxies. They were applying physics—the study of matter and energy—to heavenly bodies. Rubin was hooked. There was so much to learn! Galaxies fascinated her. How did they move? Did they rotate the way planets in the solar system do? Scientists had found that galaxies were moving outward as the universe expands. Rubin thought they were rotating around invisible centers.

In December of 1951, as she was about to have her first baby, Rubin traveled to Haverford College through a snowstorm to deliver a paper to the American Astronomical Society introducing the idea that galaxies rotated around invisible centers. (Because she was pregnant and not a member of the society, one of her advisers had offered to present it for her—in his name—but she declined.)

The all-male audience listened in silence. The discussion afterward was harshly critical. Two journals rejected Rubin's paper.

Discouraged, Rubin took refuge in motherhood. But that wasn't enough. She had a passionate calling. And fortunately, she had a very supportive husband. "I realized that as much as we both adored this child, there was nothing in my background that had led me to expect that [my husband] would go off to work each day doing what he loved to do, and I would stay home with this lovely child," she later said. "I really found it very, very hard. And it was he who insisted that I go back to school."

Cosmologist George Gamow was interested enough to oversee her doctoral thesis at Georgetown University. To have time for her children, Rubin took night classes. She didn't drive, so her husband waited for her in their car while her parents babysat. Meanwhile, she helped support her growing family by teaching at local community colleges.

the existence of dark matter

From 1965 on, Rubin conducted her research on the motion of galaxies as a staff member of the Department of Terrestrial Magnetism at the Carnegie Institute in Washington, DC. She had done earlier work on quasars—distant objects in distant galaxies that give off enormous energy, powered by black holes. They had only recently been discovered, so her work prompted other astronomers to pepper her with questions, as well as unsolicited advice. Rubin preferred to be left alone to do her work. To avoid these intrusions, she picked a subject she thought no one cared about but that would make colleagues happy when she was done. That topic was a survey of spiral galaxy rotation curves.

galaxies

Galaxies are organizations of stars, dust, and gas. Until the twentieth century, scientists believed there was only one galaxy, the Milky Way. That system and its stars seemed fixed and unchanging. Now we know there are at least four hundred billion galaxies in our universe, which constantly expands according to Newton's laws of motion. Stars are being born and dying all the time. Astronomers can see evidence of the Big Bang that began it all, but visibility is limited by the light that reaches our telescopes. Light from very far away brings information from the very distant past and takes a long time to reach our telescopes. That information has led to the idea that the universe began with a Big Bang and that most of the matter out there in the universe is dark matter.

As part of her work, Rubin was the first woman permitted to use the giant telescope at Mt. Palomar, near San Diego, in 1965. Before then, female astronomers were barred from using observatories unless accompanied by a man—"no restroom facilities" was the excuse. Rubin cut a piece of paper into a skirt shape and taped it to the male silhouette on the door of one of the men's rooms. "Now you have a ladies' room," she said.

Her collaborator at the Department of Terrestrial Magnetism was W. Kent Ford. They used an instrument called a spectrometer to measure the rotation curves of galaxies. To their surprise, they found the outer edges of the Andromeda galaxy rotated as fast as the center, violating one of Isaac Newton's laws of motion. The outer edges swirled so fast they should have flown out into space. The mass that could be seen through a telescope didn't look big enough to hold the galaxy together. After testing the idea sixty times, Rubin felt certain that some unknown substance was holding the galaxies together as they spun.

Because that substance emits no light, it came to be called *dark matter*. Going back to the early 1900s, scientists had thought there was some sort of unseen matter in the universe. In 1974, a landmark paper by Princeton physicists said that spiral galaxies would warp and fall apart unless they were embedded in dark matter, like a hamburger in a bun. It was Rubin and Ford's work through the 1970s and early 1980s that confirmed the existence of this dark matter.

At the same time, several new kinds of subatomic particles were discovered. Scientists began to realize that as much as 68 percent of matter is unknown, yet to be discovered. "We are out of kindergarten but only in third grade," Rubin once said. "I'm sorry I know so little. I'm sorry we all know so little. But that's kind of the fun, isn't it?"

dark matter

A European astrophysicist named Fritz Zwicky coined the term *dark matter*. He believed there could not be enough observable mass in the universe to explain why galaxies rotating at high speed, like so many pinwheels, held together without flying apart. He believed there must be some unseen matter exerting a gravitational influence on the matter we can observe, but he couldn't prove it. Writing in a Swiss journal in 1933, Zwicky described this mysterious matter as *dunkle materie*: dark matter. Scientists, drawing on Vera Rubin's work, now think dark matter makes up about 84 percent of the material in the universe. We can't see it because it does not absorb or give off light.

legacy

Rubin raised four children—one girl and three boys—with her husband. Their daughter became an astronomer, and all four children earned PhDs in science or math. Rubin campaigned on behalf of women scientists all her life. She mentored countless young women, offering realistic advice, never sugarcoating the difficulties. Many believe she should have been given the Nobel Prize in Physics; that was a theme of her obituaries when she died. (Only two women have ever won one.) As Emily Levesque, an astronomer at the University of Washington, said of Rubin's contribution—and her lack of a Nobel Prize: "The existence of dark matter has utterly revolutionized our concept of the universe and our entire field; the ongoing effort to understand the role of dark matter has basically spawned entire subfields within astrophysics and particle physics at this point."

Although Rubin didn't win the Nobel Prize, she was awarded other honors, including the National Medal of Science in 1993 and the Gold Medal of the Royal Astronomical Society—only the second woman to do so—in 1996. The president of the Royal Astronomical Society commented on her contribution and on all Rubin, as a woman, had to overcome to make her mark: "Vera Rubin made truly seminal discoveries in astronomy which inform the view of the universe that we hold today. Her ideas were only fully accepted many years after they were first put forward, partly because they were so groundbreaking, and partly perhaps because she was at the time one of the very few female astronomers in what was a completely male-dominated environment."

Vera Rubin died on December 25, 2016. She had urged young women, "Each one of you can change the world, for you are made of star stuff, and you are connected to the universe." So did she change our world and inspire the women who follow her.

"Don't shoot for the stars. We already know what's there. Shoot for the space in between because that's where the real mystery lies."

—vera rubin

JOAN GANZ COONEY

innovator of educational tv

1929–

For half a century, *Sesame Street* has been enchanting America's young children with its academic and social lessons. In 1968, during an era of violent, dreary, half-hearted kids' programming, Joan Ganz Cooney saw that TV could be used creatively to prepare disadvantaged youngsters for school—and for life. *Sesame Street* shaped a new kind of instructive entertainment. On the show, Jim Henson's Muppets became beloved companions who embodied good values, such as sharing and respecting others. *Sesame Street* was an instant success and has remained so. Cooney succeeded in meeting the goal she set for herself as a teenager: to truly make a difference.

joan ganz was born on November 30, 1929, in Phoenix, Arizona—just in time, as she puts it, for the Great Depression, when many people were out of work and hungry. The Depression hardly affected her childhood, though, which had an "upper-class, country club atmosphere," she recalls. Her father was a banker and her mother a homemaker. She was expected to follow in her mother's footsteps.

a born idealist

But Joan described herself as a "driven, idealistic kid." Her mind was set alight by a high school teacher who led discussions about poverty, a free press, and anti-Semitism (hatred of Jewish people) in Germany under Hitler. World War II had revealed genocide (the attempt to eliminate whole peoples), caused widespread destruction in Europe and Asia, and resulted in the first use of an atomic bomb. Afterward, leaders were asking how a better world could be created to ensure that such evil would not occur again. As a teenager, Joan eagerly grappled with such profound questions and was determined to find a way to make a difference. But it wasn't yet clear how.

She performed in plays in high school and at the University of Arizona, but when her father refused to support her in a theatrical career, she reluctantly abandoned acting. Instead, she majored in education. She had no interest in teaching but had found it was one of the few acceptable jobs for women at that time. Still, she wouldn't passively pursue a career she wasn't interested in; after all, her college nickname was "Guts."

After graduating in 1951, Joan worked as a typist for a year at the US State Department. In Washington, DC, she became aware of a Catholic group called the Christophers and their founder, Father James Keller. He preached religious tolerance and used television to get out the message. Keller urged young idealists to go to work in media—or else, he warned, non-idealists would dominate it.

Joan took that message to heart, returning to Arizona to work as a reporter on the *Arizona Republic*.

But she hadn't yet found the right outlet for her talents. In 1953, she moved to New York, intending to find a job in public relations. She soon found herself at a party attended by David Sarnoff, the head of Radio Corporation of America (RCA), which owned the broadcasting company NBC. She impressed him so favorably, he found her a job in the company's public information department. There, she wrote soap opera summaries for a time. Then a better job came along: public relations for the sponsor of the popular dramatic television program *The United States Steel Hour*.

finding her true calling

Outside work, Joan befriended a group of left-leaning writers and intellectuals who met for evening discussions. Some of them introduced her to the reform arm of the New York Democratic Party. She made important connections there with people who could share her commitment to social change through media.

In 1961, she learned that a New York nonprofit group was taking over a faltering independent station, Channel 13. It looked to Joan like a golden opportunity to put her ideals to work. She applied to be public relations director for the station. The manager told her they didn't need one. Since the scant budget allowed only for talk shows and low-cost documentaries, what they needed was a producer. Joan boldly said she could produce documentaries, despite not knowing anything about the work, and they hired her.

She turned out to be very good at the job. The award-winning films Joan produced—*Poverty, Anti-Poverty, and the Poor* and *A Chance at the Beginning*, about a Harlem preschool program that preceded Head Start—helped establish Channel 13 as a top provider of public interest television. Her work opened

Joan's eyes to the dire need for early childhood education, especially for disadvantaged children.

Finally immersed in a satisfying career, Joan was ready to marry. Timothy Cooney, whom she wed in 1964, was a director of public relations for the New York City Department of Labor. He supported her ambitions and believed in the causes she was exploring in film. "My husband made me a feminist," Joan said. He became a volunteer advocating for the poor, making Joan the sole breadwinner of the family, which eventually included an African American foster child.

One night, in 1966, the Cooneys gave a dinner party. Among the guests was a vice president of the Carnegie Foundation, which funded education. The discussion turned to the low quality of television programming for children: mostly cartoons, commercials, and the occasional book show with still shots of illustrations. Could television be used to educate children, the guests wondered?

The foundation executive said he'd found his two little children watching test patterns while waiting for cartoons to come on. That was the power of the television set! Joan realized she was being presented with just the kind of opportunity she'd been waiting for. Of course, she said, TV could be a medium for education.

sesame street

The next day the executive called and asked her to research and write a report on the subject. Joan agreed. She traveled the nation, interviewing experts and children and studying the impact of television on them. The report she produced was called "The Potential Uses of Television in Preschool

Education." Along with data from psychologists and educators, it included her own recommendations: A children's show must be visually colorful, fast moving, and full of action, humor, and music. It should have a permanent host and be broadcast twice a day for one hour. Cooney noted that children loved commercials, especially jingles. Why not have commercials for letters and numbers? Finally, the show had to be sophisticated enough for parents to watch along with their kids.

The idea for a show was presented to the big networks, NBC and CBS, but they passed. So Cooney returned to her home base, public broadcasting.

Channel 13 didn't have the resources to put it together, but Cooney gathered funds from foundations. The federal government's War on Poverty had demonstrated that disadvantaged children desperately needed a head start in education. The various foundations and the Department of Education eagerly pitched in with the millions needed. A new company, the Children's Television Workshop, was created to be the show's producer.

Elements of the show were tested in day care centers with great success. The children were entertained—and they learned. The psychedelic graphics popular in the 1960s captured their attention. One of the producers suggested using Jim Henson's Muppets, a group of funny and lovable puppets that appeared on another TV show. Henson was reluctant to be identified with a children's production, but his Muppets were already popular—"hip and edgy," Joan recalled. He got on board. One expert warned they shouldn't mix fantasy and reality. But test audiences, who had found the street set dreary, loved it when puppets were added. *Sesame Street* was named for the magic word that opens a cave filled with treasure in the ancient story "Ali Baba and the Forty Thieves."

Before the show went on the air, Cooney was told that the producers were looking for a man to be the executive director of Children's Television Workshop (CTW). She would be his second-in-command. Encouraged by her husband, Cooney refused to be number two. She told them she had to be number one, and they finally agreed and gave her the top position. "It was absolutely what I was born to do and I knew it," Joan said.

The first show aired on November 10, 1969, and was an immediate sensation. People called *Sesame Street* a miracle for children. Cooney visited PBS (Public Broadcasting Service) outlets all over the country and persuaded them to air the show.

There were a few critics. At first, Jim Henson didn't think women could handle the physical work of puppetry, and the show's creators worried that girl characters who made kids laugh might seem like stereotypes. As a result, there were no female characters for a while. Mothers and women's groups objected, and eventually, female puppeteers and Muppets were added. Some observers worried the jumpy psychedelics would cause seizures. Others accused the program of pushing rote learning that wouldn't stick. But they were a tiny minority. Research showed that the program was extraordinarily effective. Preschoolers who watched *Sesame Street* were more likely to be academically prepared for school and advance through their educational paths at rates appropriate for their age.

Gradually, more social lessons were introduced: fighting racism by way of Kermit, who found it hard to be green, and tolerating imperfection by Big Bird, whose many mistakes were forgiven. Affection for these characters linked American children across all geographic and cultural lines.

an american institution

The show won numerous awards. Success brought expansion. A second show, *The Electric Company*, stressing reading for eight- to twelve-year-olds, was launched in 1971. Several other specialized programs followed. Children's Television Workshop, which produced them, became Sesame Workshop. And in 2015, *Sesame Street* was sold to HBO, where it now airs.

Joan Ganz Cooney continued to lead the organization until 1990, when she became chair of the executive board. Those who worked under her called her a strong and flexible boss. She spoke out about education issues, advocating, for example, a longer school day and year and more creative use of television. She had little patience for those who simply criticize the medium and don't try to use it well. Because *Sesame Street* and its offshoots weren't funded by commercials, Cooney constantly had to raise money and make sure the programs didn't stray from their original vision. ("It's terribly wrong to be pitching products at the young," she said in explaining why *Sesame Street* could never rely on ads. "It's like shooting fish in a barrel. It's grotesquely unfair.")

staying relevant

In March 2017 *Sesame Street* introduced Julia, an orange-haired, green-eyed four-year-old who likes to paint and pick flowers, and who often echoes what she's just heard her friends say. Julia has autism, a condition that includes difficulty communicating and relating to others, and sensitivity to sensory stimulation.

With Julia, *Sesame Street* aims to help destigmatize autism, which affects about one in sixty-eight American children. The episode—part of a plan to support families with autistic children, called *See Amazing in All Children*—is supplemented by books and other materials.

Sherrie Westin, who oversaw the plan, tells of the impact: "One of my favorite stories is a mother who said that she used the book to explain to her child that she had autism like Julia. This became the tool for her to have a conversation with her five-year-old daughter. And you'll love this. At the end, her daughter said, 'So I'm amazing, too, right?'"

Cooney was admitted to the TV Hall of Fame in 1990. She was given the Presidential Medal of Freedom by Bill Clinton in 1995. The Children's Television Workshop under her leadership won numerous awards, including the Emmy. *Sesame Street* reaches some one hundred million children and families in more than 150 countries.

Joan Ganz Cooney changed the landscape of children's television programming. In doing that, she provided millions of children with the tools to improve their chances for success in life.

"There were people who were sure we were absolutely destroying the minds of children, but they were drowned out. . . . Nothing like [Sesame Street] had ever been seen before."

—joan ganz cooney

DOLORES HUERTA

the labor organizer
who said "Yes, we can!"

1930–

Dolores Huerta, a Latinx American labor organizer and educator, is still working to change the world for the better. Born during the Depression when money was tight, she knew mistreated migrant workers and felt the sting of discrimination herself. Huerta was determined to fight for the right of everyone to earn a decent wage. Together with Cesar Chavez, she founded the United Farm Workers. The strikes and the boycotts of table grapes and lettuce organized by the union won major victories for farmworkers in the 1960s and '70s. Huerta's work changed the way Americans felt about the people who harvested their food. With her courage and eloquence, she changed people's minds about women's roles, too.

dolores fernandez was born on April 10, 1930, in Dawson,

New Mexico, a mining town. Her father, Juan, labored in a mine and on farms. Life was hard for the family, but he was committed to helping his fellow workers. Like her parents, Dolores was steeped in the culture and politics of the Latinx community.

When she was three, her parents divorced and she moved with her mother, Alicia, and two brothers to Stockton, California, another community of farmworkers. Back in New Mexico, Juan Fernandez organized workers for a union—an association formed to protect the workers' rights. He was also elected to state office. Although geography separated Dolores from her father, she was inspired by his life and work.

finding her way

Dolores's mother struggled to support her children. Eventually she prospered enough to open a restaurant and hotel for migrant workers. She allowed people to stay and eat even when they couldn't pay. At home, she made culture and education priorities, managing to find the money to afford such privileges as music and dance lessons for the children. Her hard work and her values were an inspiration to her daughter.

Dolores played the violin and piano, danced, and was a Girl Scout and a drum majorette. She was a talented writer, as well. But one day in high school, a teacher accused her of plagiarism. The teacher assumed a Latina lacked the ability to write well in English. Dolores knew it was racial bias.

She also witnessed violent police attacks on immigrants, many of them her friends. Her instinct already was to find a way to fight back.

But first she fell in love, got married, had two children, and was divorced, all before she graduated from college. She taught school for a while but gave it up because her students, the children of migrant workers, were too hungry to pay attention. She needed to find another way to address their problems.

"I couldn't tolerate seeing kids come to class hungry and needing shoes," Huerta later said. "I thought I could do more by organizing farmworkers than by trying to teach their hungry children."

community organizing

Her life changed when she met Fred Ross, a charismatic community organizer. He started the local Stockton chapter of the Community Services Organization (CSO), a grassroots group dedicated to ending segregation and police brutality. Fred had managed to have police put in jail for beating up Latinx people. Dolores helped lead the Stockton CSO. She registered voters and lobbied the all-white male legislature to provide public assistance to workers who were not citizens.

She married a fellow activist named Ventura Huerta and eventually had five more children with him. They campaigned together for a law to protect the civil rights of Spanish-speaking workers. For her, it was an emotional crusade. She never forgot the dirt floors she saw when she visited one farmworker's ramshackle home. How could society ignore the needs of the hardworking people who provided its food?

teaming up with cesar chavez

In 1960, Dolores Huerta formed a group called the Agricultural Workers Association (AWA), which was devoted to helping farmworkers. She had also met Cesar Chavez, the director of the CSO. They realized they had a common goal.

Together Huerta and Chavez would change the course of labor history. In 1962, she and Chavez left the AWA and CSO and founded the National Farm Workers Association. Chavez was president and Huerta vice president. He was the dynamic speaker, and she was the organizer and tough negotiator. (In time, she became a dynamic speaker in her own right.) They adopted the slogan *Viva la Causa!* (*Long live the cause*). Huerta urged women to take active roles in the organization and demanded that they be treated as equals by the men. By then, she had seven children. To do her work she often had to leave them in the care of others.

california farmworkers

Farm work in California has historically been done by temporary laborers—most of them immigrants—who roam the state looking for jobs. In the mid-twentieth century, landowners hired companies to handle the hiring, paying, and firing of their workers. They always hired about 40 percent more individuals than were needed. That meant workers had to compete for jobs and got lower pay. A great many nationalities were represented—Chinese, Filipino, Indian— on large farms that raised animals in factory-like conditions. By the time Huerta and Chavez began their work, many workers were Mexican.

The federal Civil Rights Act, banning discrimination on the basis of race and sex, had passed in 1964. It was a good time to fight for the rights of immigrant workers, too. In 1965, the Farm Workers Association joined a strike against rose growers. Workers on the farms had to graft the roses. The job involved crawling down rows of thousands of plants, cutting slits in the stems, and inserting buds. The pay was supposed to be nine dollars for every thousand grafts, but the farmworkers usually got only seven dollars. Huerta gathered workers together and told them to touch a crucifix and promise not to break the strike. They all promised. The strike was a success. The owner signed a contract raising wages within a week.

the grape boycott

Huerta and Chavez next tackled California's grape growers. Grape pickers worked without toilets or even drinking water in the hot vineyards. A group of Filipino grape pickers in Delano, California, had stopped working to protest their low wages. Chavez and Huerta rallied the Mexican grape pickers, and in 1965, all of them went on strike. The organizers demanded a reduction in the use of dangerous chemical pesticides, higher pay, and unemployment and health benefits for the workers.

The owners fought back, unleashing attack dogs on the striking workers, spraying thick dust and pesticides on them, and sending thugs to beat them up. The owners hired thousands of non-union substitute Mexican workers, known as *scabs*, to continue the harvest. But Huerta went to El Paso, where the new workers were streaming across the border, and handed out leaflets asking them not to work for the Delano grape growers. Many came anyway, but not all. Finally in 1966, one grower agreed to a new contract. Huerta negotiated the terms and signed it for the union, which was now called the United Farm Workers.

There was much more to do. Huerta went to New York City, a major distribution point for grapes. Her mission was to persuade stores to stop selling and consumers to stop buying table grapes. If enough people took part in this boycott, the growers would have to agree to better working conditions. She went to work organizing a coalition of student, religious, labor, feminist, and consumer groups, crossing racial, ethnic, and class lines to pressure stores not to sell grapes. The boycott was a success. Huerta kept the strike in the news, and grapes stayed off many Americans' tables for years.

The strike was supported by 1968 presidential candidate Robert F. Kennedy. RFK, as he was known, became close with Huerta and Chavez. Many hoped a second Kennedy administration—following that of RFK's brother, the assassinated President John F. Kennedy—would improve the lot of immigrant workers. That spring, Huerta was with RFK when he, too, was shot dead in Los Angeles after winning the California primary. The union was devastated by the loss, as were many other Americans.

The strike lasted five years, and eventually the boycott extended to lettuce and Gallo wine, to protect those workers as well. Throughout, the growers used violence to intimidate the strikers. But in the end, the farmworkers won. Huerta's negotiating skill led to a provision in the contract banning the pesticide DDT, well before it was banned by the federal government. During this campaign she invented the slogan *Sí se puede*, which means *Yes, we can!* (Years later, at a White House ceremony honoring Huerta, President Barack Obama would admit that his campaign had "stolen" the phrase from her. Before that, people had credited Cesar Chavez with coining the slogan.)

strikes

America saw growth in factories and manufacturing jobs in the nineteenth century. As large factories were built, people moved to cities to find jobs. Many had worked on their own small farms or had been craftspeople who managed their own work. Now the factory owners and foremen had complete power over the workers. If workers wanted higher wages or better conditions, the only way they could pressure their bosses was to stop working—to strike. When strikes were called, workers stayed home and hoped the owners would give in to their demands. When workers banded together in unions, the strike was their best tool for persuading owners to improve working conditions and raise pay.

a never-ending fight

In 1975, the California state legislature passed the Agricultural Labor Relations Act. For the first time, the right of farmworkers to gather together and bargain on behalf of their group was protected by law. It was a great victory for farmworkers but was one of the last. After 1980, the Reagan administration pushed policies that weakened labor unions, and they have never recovered.

But Dolores Huerta went on fighting.

During the 1960s and '70s, she was arrested twenty-two times while striking and protesting working conditions. During a violent attempt by the Teamsters Union to take over the United Farm Workers, her house was vandalized and people pointed guns at her and her family. She never wavered. During the 1980s, she campaigned for fair immigration laws, better health conditions for farmworkers, and women's rights. In 1988, she took part in a rally at a fundraiser in San Francisco against the policies of presidential candidate George H. W. Bush and was beaten so badly by a police officer she nearly died.

As she grew older, her activism took the form of lecture tours and writing. Feminism became a signature issue. In 1991, she went around the country seeking Latina women to run for office. In 1998, *Ms.* magazine named her Woman of the Year.

In 1993, she became the first Latina woman inducted into the National Women's Hall of Fame. That year also brought great sadness. She lost her partner and friend when Cesar Chavez died. Dolores Huerta delivered the eulogy at his funeral.

In 1998, Huerta was awarded the Eleanor Roosevelt Award for Human Rights by President Bill Clinton. The next year she retired from the United Farm Workers. But she didn't stop working. In 2002, she led a 165-mile march to the California state capitol to pressure government to enact new laws protecting workers. And that year she received the Puffin/Nation Prize for Creative Citizenship, given to someone who "has challenged the status quo through distinctive, courageous, imaginative, and socially responsible work of significance." She used the $100,000 award to establish the Dolores Huerta Foundation. Its mission is to train citizens from low-income communities to organize in order to make their voices heard. As the foundation trains activists, Huerta continues to speak out about income inequality, immigration, and the rights of Latinxs and women. She received the Presidential Medal of Freedom from President Obama in 2012.

Farmworkers were the forgotten people. Dolores Huerta brought them and their harsh lives into the light. She helped forge the tools to force growers to treat them more fairly. At the age of eighty-eight, she is still speaking forcefully and eloquently for justice and equality.

"And I want to say to mothers out there, you know, take your children to marches. Take them to meetings because this is a way that they can become strong, and they understand what politics is all about because they are actually living it."

—dolores huerta

BARBARA GITTINGS

mother of the gay rights movement

1932–2007

After finding common cause with other lesbians, nearly all of them "in the closet" (not declaring their sexual orientation), Barbara Gittings led a militant movement to make life better—and more honest—for all in her community. She picketed, staged protests, wrote articles, and invaded government and corporate offices to demand civil rights for gay women and men. She led the charge to have gay people work for the government, to stock libraries with books providing helpful information about homosexuality, and to remove homosexuality from the list of official psychiatric disorders. Having struggled for self-acceptance as a young woman, she devoted her life to acceptance and equal rights for all gay women and men.

barbara brooks gittings was born in 1932 in Vienna,

Austria, where her father was stationed as a diplomat. He was a devout Catholic, her mother was a convert, and their children attended parochial schools. "My life was so steeped in . . . Catholicism," Gittings said, "that for a time I wanted to become a nun." She didn't feel comfortable in her family, nor was she comfortable at school.

Her family returned to the United States in the 1940s, with the outbreak of World War II, and moved to Wilmington, Delaware. In eighth grade, she developed a serious crush on another girl, who did not reciprocate. A teacher told Barbara she might be "homosexual." Barbara had never heard of such a thing. Adding to her confusion, the object of her crush, distressed by the rumors about them, stopped speaking to her. Then Barbara was denied membership in an honor society because of "character." She didn't connect their comment about "character" with homosexuality until later in life.

Barbara had discovered that lesbian novels offered some comfort. Her father found a book about lesbian love in her bedroom. Unwilling to confront her in person, he wrote her a letter ordering her to burn the book. She refused.

a tormented self-discovery

Gittings enrolled at Northwestern University in Chicago, where she had a short relationship with a woman and was again the subject of rumors about her homosexuality. By then, she was desperate to find out if it was true—and what it meant. She used her allowance to pay for an appointment with a psychiatrist who told Barbara that she was indeed gay and offered a lengthy and expensive treatment to attempt to "cure" her. At the time, homosexuality was defined as a mental illness, deviant and abnormal. Doctors attempted to treat it with electric shock therapy, psychotherapy, and medical procedures.

But instead of accepting the treatment, Barbara instantly accepted the label. She was relieved to have the matter settled and wanted only to know more about it. She began to research homosexuality in libraries. There was no other way to find out about it, as it was not openly discussed in society or the media. Most of the books she consulted described homosexuality as abnormal and perverted. After months of reading, she was still perplexed. Having spent all her time in libraries instead of in classes, she flunked out of college.

Barbara had read that gay people got together in bars. She hitchhiked to New York City dressed as a boy and wandered into Greenwich Village bars, carrying a novel so she'd have something to talk about. She didn't like the atmosphere of those places and didn't drink, but as she later said, it was the only way to find other gay people. But she found the bars were unwelcoming, and the women she met weren't interested in literature.

At eighteen, Barbara moved to a rooming house in Philadelphia. She got a job and joined a choir. After a few months, her father wrote her again, this time to say he forgave her. But she never went back home.

becoming a revolutionary

For the next few years, Barbara worked at a music store and an architectural firm. Her search to understand homosexuality led her to the Mattachine Society, a gay rights organization whose members were mostly men. They told her about the Daughters of Bilitis (DOB), the first organization in the United States for lesbians, which was founded in 1955 in California. Gittings traveled to California to meet the women activists and was thrilled to find they met in living rooms, not bars. She had found her own community at last!

Although DOB's approach was too conservative for Barbara—it urged lesbians to try to fit into society and not to assert themselves in ways that might offend anyone—she returned to New York and in 1958 started the first East Coast branch of DOB, serving as president. In 1961, Barbara met Kay Tobin Lahusen, a photographer whose own search for a lesbian community had brought her to DOB. They fell in love and were life partners until Barbara died.

DOB put out a magazine called the *Ladder*, which was sent through the mail in a plain brown envelope. Had it been openly mailed, the post office would have confiscated it and possibly charged the organization with obscenity. Barbara became editor of the *Ladder* in 1963. She was already helping to shape a movement.

The *Ladder*'s cover had always featured drawings. Kay suggested they run photographs of actual lesbians. This act was an early version of "coming out," showing the human face of homosexuality. The purpose of DOB was to integrate lesbians into society, not to prolong their isolation from it. The public, too, had to be educated—and laws discriminating against gays and lesbians had to be changed.

a powerful ally

In 1957, Frank Kameny, an astronomer with the US Army Map Service, was fired for being gay. Kameny sued the government. He lost but asked the US Supreme Court to direct that the case be considered again. It refused, but his was the first civil rights claim based on sexual orientation to reach the nation's highest court. What's more, his case launched a decades-long battle against the government's discriminatory policies. His then-radical position was that in the absence of any real scientific evidence, gays and lesbians were not "sick," as "experts" maintained. Instead, they were as normal as heterosexuals; they just had a different sexual preference.

Gittings sided with Kameny in the debate. In August 1964, she published an editorial in the *Ladder* protesting the New York Academy of Medicine's designation of homosexuality as a disease. The academy's stance was, the editorial said, a "sly, desperate trend to enforce conformity." But the West Coast head of research for DOB disagreed. Lesbians, she said, were not experts and should listen to people who were: psychiatrists. In 1965, Gittings ran a debate between Kameny and the West Coast researcher in the *Ladder*.

The tide was turning. The gay person's problem could no longer be dismissed as psychological—it was political and social. But it wouldn't be easy to change minds. In 1966, *Time* magazine featured an article called "The Homosexual in America," calling gayness a "pernicious sickness." Kay and Barbara shot back in the *Ladder* that *Time*'s analysis was simply wrong. This was too much for the DOB head office. Both women were fired from the magazine.

militants for change

Gittings was ready to leave DOB. She had already begun to take public actions to fight for gay rights. Frank Kameny was just one of thousands of federal workers who had lost their jobs and had their lives ruined because they were gay. Taking their cue from the Civil Rights Movement and the second-wave feminists, Kameny and Gittings marched with protest signs outside federal buildings in Washington, DC. A protest by them and others outside the White House in April 1965 is believed to be the first major gay rights demonstration.

The issues were that gays and lesbians were barred from working for the government and serving in the armed forces and that they were denied security clearances. Gay people had been somewhat shielded by the fact that, unlike Black people and women, they didn't look different from other folks. It took courage to "come out" and march openly, but a few dozen did—week after week after week. Gittings always dressed for the occasion in a dress, stockings, and little heels. She wanted people to focus on the message, not the messenger, although she did harbor some misgivings about having to look so conventional.

Completely comfortable in her own skin, she easily reached out to others. Her big smile, sense of humor, and dedication made her a popular leader. And she was seemingly inexhaustible.

stonewall

Throughout the 1950s and '60s, police regularly raided gay bars, seizing alcohol, shutting down establishments, and arresting patrons suspected of being gay. It wasn't uncommon for gay men and lesbians to be exposed in newspapers, fired from their jobs, jailed, or sent to mental institutions.

Then on June 28, 1969, police entered the Stonewall Inn, a gay bar in New York's Greenwich Village, at 1:20 a.m. and launched a raid that would galvanize the gay rights movement.

While the police waited for patrol wagons to cart away the arrested suspects, the bar's patrons began to resist. They refused to follow police orders. Those who weren't arrested exited through the front door, but they didn't go far. Within a short time, the crowd swelled to an estimated two thousand people. As police put the arrested women and men into the wagons that were now on the scene, the crowd threw what they had—pennies, beer bottles, trash cans—at the police and shouted, "Gay power!"

This first major protest on behalf of equal rights for homosexuals brought together the gay community in a way nothing had previously, leading to the formation of thousands of gay rights organizations and powerful change.

Gittings and Kameny became advisors to gays fired from their jobs. She was beginning to acquire the reputation of "mother of the gay rights movement." They both appeared at Pentagon hearings dressed conservatively, as usual. Gittings and Kameny were present to observe when the FBI grilled fired gay workers. And they made sure reporters covered these events. They argued that in every case, nothing in employees' private lives made them security risks or unfit for work.

the homosexual "disease"

After Stonewall, Gittings decided to let the radicals fight for gay liberation in their own way. She had again taken up a long-held cause: how doctors viewed homosexuality. When the American Psychological Association (APA) met in Boston in 1968, Gittings had gone undercover, listening as practitioners uttered preposterous assumptions about "crazy" homosexuals.

She began pressuring the association to hold hearings about their definition of homosexuality. In 1972, after dogged persistence, she and some colleagues were permitted to set up a booth at an APA meeting. Gittings took a theatrical approach: She labeled the booth Gay Proud and Healthy and covered it with photographs of gay and lesbian couples. Behind it was a kissing booth, a giant LOVE adorning the front. Gittings couldn't persuade any doctors to take part in a panel discussion she'd organized. Finally, a closeted psychiatrist agreed to do it wearing a Nixon mask. The result was a sensation. In 1973, the APA voted to remove homosexuality from its manual of psychiatric disorders. In time, homosexuality was no longer described as a disease by other respected medical, psychiatric, and psychological associations.

Gittings's final crusade was, she said, to "counter the lies in the libraries about homosexuality so that gay people [would] no longer be assaulted or bewildered or demoralized by almost everything they read on the subject." As a young girl, she'd looked for solace in library books and instead found herself labeled "perverted." She turned again to books, compiling an extensive bibliography about homosexuality. Since literature, scientific and otherwise, about homosexuality is now very different from what it was then, we can say for sure that Gittings's efforts were successful.

In 1973, Barbara cofounded the National Gay Task Force, which encouraged homosexual people to publicly declare their orientation. It also helped make gay men and women a significant voting bloc in elections.

Gittings remained an active figure into the 1990s, almost until she died on February 18, 2007. During one of her many appearances on television, she said, "Homosexuals today are taking it for granted that their homosexuality is not at all something dreadful—it's good, it's right, it's natural, it's moral, and this is the way it's going to be!"

She was right. And that happy fact was very much due to her own courage and persistence in making the truth known.

"We are defining our own lives for ourselves, we are setting our own expectations for ourselves, we're developing our own value systems. This is what it's about. You can't force us into your boxes any more, we are not going."

—barbara gittings

BILLIE JEAN KING

champion for sports and equality

1943–

Billie Jean King ignited a revolution in women's sports. Playing tennis was what she did best, and she wanted to earn a living doing it. But in the 1960s, professional tennis was a man's game. While men could earn a living playing tennis, women's prize money was just a fraction of the men's. As King won tournament after tournament, rising to the top of women's tennis, she fought for comparable pay. In 1973, she coolly defeated tennis star Bobby Riggs before forty-eight million television viewers. The Battle of the Sexes match instantly raised the status of all women players, as Billie knew it would. Thanks to her, women's tennis became a profession. The World Tour she founded has discovered and nurtured countless gifted young athletes. She continues to devote her generous heart and boundless energy to social justice.

billie jean moffitt was born in Long Beach, California, in 1943. The Moffitts were a family of athletes, and Billie Jean, exceptionally good at every ball sport, set her sights on becoming a professional baseball player. But while watching a professional game one day, it suddenly dawned on her that there were no women on the field. Her dream was clearly impossible. There weren't any women in football or basketball either.

If team sports were out, why not tennis? Billie Jean asked her parents for a racket. The Moffitts found a public court that offered group lessons. (Tennis was typically a sport played at country clubs, and the Kings could not afford the membership fees.) After her first lesson, eleven-year-old Billie Jean excitedly told her mother she had found what she wanted to do with her life.

Tennis is a game of the mind as well as the body. From the beginning, Billie Jean showed remarkable mental focus and skill—along with a strong drive to win.

On the public courts that were her training ground, young Billie Jean was again struck by inequality. "I looked around and I saw that everyone who plays wears white socks, white shoes, a white tennis dress or shorts, and they're all white," she later said. "My question to myself was: Where is everybody else? There are no people of color. Something's not right."

Billie Jean was white, but she was an outsider in the tennis world because she wasn't from a wealthy family. At eleven, she was barred from the group photo at a tournament because she was wearing shorts her mother had made for her, not a standard tennis skirt.

But with her skill and competitive spirit, she began to rise through the ranks. The Moffitts couldn't afford to fly her to distant matches, so she often arrived exhausted from long bus or car trips. Still, she won.

A wealthy supporter arranged to pay for coaching from Alice Marble, a

Wimbledon star with a fast, aggressive game. She advanced Billie Jean's game so that she was ranked the #19 women's tennis player by the US Lawn Tennis Association.

Two years later, Billie Jean and her partner were the youngest pair in history to win the doubles title at Wimbledon, a famous tennis championship held in England since 1877. Billie Jean adored Wimbledon with its strict traditions, perhaps because it was so historic. On the courts there she felt completely at home. And she returned year after year.

the grand slam tournaments

Tennis has four major championship tournaments, each played over a two-week period and each more than one hundred years old. They are the Australian Open, the French Open, Wimbledon, and the US Open. Players who win titles in all four of the tournaments in one year are called Grand Slam winners. Billie Jean King won thirty-nine different Grand Slam tournaments.

She was #3 in the national rankings when she enrolled in Los Angeles State College. Her boyfriend, Larry King, had a tennis scholarship. But it was 1961 and no colleges offered athletic scholarships for women.

Billie Jean and her boyfriend both thought it was very unfair. "You know you're a second-class citizen, right?" she recalls Larry saying. "Because you're a girl."

She and King married, and he became her biggest supporter and manager, through the thick and thin of an imperfect marriage. King already knew she was attracted to women, but she was ashamed of those feelings.

Despite the uncertainty in her personal life, Billie Jean went on winning—doubles at Wimbledon in 1963 and the singles title in 1966. The next year she won all three Wimbledon titles: singles, doubles, and mixed doubles (in which a man and woman play as a team). Her single-minded drive to be the best impressed everyone who saw her play. "I expect to win every time I step on a tennis court," she said.

founding women's tennis

In spite of all her victories, Billie Jean was unable to make a living doing what she did best: tennis. For that to happen, people had to take women's tennis seriously, and its players needed to be paid well. In 1968, the first year that women received prize money, King won $1,800 for the Wimbledon crown. The male winner got $4,800. When a US tournament offered the woman champion $1,500 and the man $12,500, King and eight other top women players refused to compete. Instead, they organized their own women's-only tournament.

King and her group, the Original Nine, struggled for two years to succeed. The National Tennis Association vigorously opposed the idea of women's-only tournaments. The women drove to any city that had a big enough stadium, and they would stop passing cars to hand out tickets to their matches. The strategy worked. In 1971, the year King won the US Open, she was the first woman athlete to earn $100,000 in a year.

"Money is everything in sports. It made me a star," she said. Money, which got the public's attention, was the route to equality.

teamwork

King used stardom to advocate tirelessly for all women players. She realized early on that enthusiasm for sports and athletes could win people over to ideas they might otherwise oppose.

In 1972, she appeared on the cover of *Sports Illustrated* as Sportswoman of the Year, a first for the magazine. "I knew [it] would be a start for women," she said. "If I made it, you can make it." The following year, when she took the singles, doubles, and mixed doubles championships at Wimbledon, King helped organize a union for women players. The time was ripe. People in the second-wave feminist movement (see page 247) had been campaigning for equal rights for a decade. Title IX, the law prohibiting sex discrimination in any federally funded education program or activity, including athletics, had just passed.

Plenty of men felt threatened by these advances. It looked to them not as if women were gaining, but as if men were losing. That was the view of a former tennis champion named Bobby Riggs, who was proud to call himself a "sexist pig." He realized the attention given women's tennis presented a money-making opportunity. Proclaiming himself a defender of men, he challenged Margaret Court, who in 1970 had won the singles Grand Slam, to play him. Court had no interest in feminism, but she leaped at the chance to earn a big cash prize.

Billie Jean King, who had declined Riggs's first challenge, told Court she had to win: "You have no idea how important this match is." Court was unmoved. When Riggs presented her with roses before the match, she curtsied. King was appalled. "She should have smacked him over the head with them," King said. "She didn't get it."

Court underestimated Riggs's ability to throw her off her game, and he easily defeated her. Crowing, he repeated his challenge to Billie Jean King. She realized now that she had to take him on. Court's defeat couldn't be allowed to stand. It kept women as second-class citizens. King firmly believed there was no reason that a fit, strong woman player couldn't defeat a man.

battle of the sexes

The Battle of the Sexes was held at the Houston Astrodome on September 20, 1973. King was twenty-nine, Riggs was fifty-five. As King said, "So much was going on to make women feel things were changing in the world. But in their own lives, not much had changed. . . . That's what made this match huge. Huge!" She had always pledged to wrest tennis from the grip of rich white men. Here was her chance to play for something much bigger than herself. She trained hard, spending the last two weeks in what she called a "zone," developing her focus.

Not all women supported her. In a bathroom stall before the match, King overheard women players betting that Riggs would win. Their lack of solidarity stung, but she emerged to confront them.

King knew that if she lost, people would not take women seriously. That made it the most important contest of her career. Her strategy was to make him run until he was exhausted. It worked.

King's defeat of Bobby Riggs in 1973 brought the women's liberation movement into the mainstream and gave it a face that people could identify with. As she observed, "It's easier to change attitudes through sports." Hers was a victory for all girls. Parents, especially fathers, began thinking their daughters as well as their sons could be athletes, and treated them accordingly.

beyond tennis

King's insistence on professionalism turned women's tennis, like big-time men's sports, into a high-stakes business, ruled by money. She acknowledged that the size of her prize determined her worth in the eyes of fans but didn't regret that. It was a fact of life.

Now she began to wonder: How could there be equality between men's and women's programs when so much money was invested in men's teams?

Some people argued for increasing funding for same-sex programs. But the National Organization for Women (NOW) and Billie Jean King proposed that gifted girls be allowed to compete with boys. True integration would mean a radical overhaul of sports and would require ending "weaker sex" laws that supposedly protected girls from injury. "I see the day coming in sports when we will all be competing on the basis of our individual abilities, not our gender," King said.

sponsorship in professional sports

Forbes magazine has called sports sponsorships "arguably the most important weapon in the more than $100 billion world of advertising." For decades, companies have paid sports teams and players to display or wear their logos as a form of advertising. Athletes can earn as much or even more money from sponsors than they do by competing. But companies are quick to withdraw their sponsorship when they don't like something an athlete says or does. That's what happened to Billie Jean King after she revealed she was a lesbian.

After winning six Wimbledon and four US Open titles, King gave up playing singles in 1975. She continued to play doubles for three more years, sometimes very well and sometimes without her old focus. After losing at Wimbledon in 1983, she concentrated on shaping the future of women's sports. She and Larry, now divorced, remained business partners and founded World Tennis. A coed professional league, it grooms young players—Venus and Serena Williams among them—in clinics around the country.

The 1980s were a painful period in her life as King began to acknowledge her sexual orientation. Her parents were slow to accept it. Still, she eventually "embraced gay pride with gusto," as one biographer put it. By the late 1990s, King was ready to use her celebrity to raise funds to end the AIDS crisis. Together with her longtime friend, singer Elton John, she has helped to raise millions of dollars to fight the disease.

On August 28, 2006, the United States Tennis Association in Flushing, New York, chose to give King its highest, most historic honor: the center where the US Open is played every year was renamed the Billie Jean King National Tennis Center. John McEnroe, tennis champion and commentator, called King the most important person in the history of women's sports. Naming a stadium for a woman rather than a corporation was remarkable.

King keeps up her activism on many fronts. She took part in Michelle Obama's Let's Move program to fight child obesity. In 2009, President Obama awarded her the Presidential Medal of Freedom. She continues to campaign for gay rights, and her foundation promotes leadership and fitness for women and girls.

The next time you watch a women's tennis match, think of the courageous woman who made their careers possible. On or off the court, Billie Jean King played to win.

*"Tennis has always been reserved for
the rich, the white, the males—
and I've always been pledged
to change all that."*

—billie jean king

ALICE
WATERS

crusader for slow food, and
founder of the edible schoolyard

1944–

*Alice Waters wants to change America for the better.
She has begun with the food we eat, because food is
the essence of life. Protect the land food grows on,
she urges. Respect the growers and share their bounty
with others in simple, delicious meals. Her crusade
began almost fifty years ago with a little restaurant
where she could feed her friends the kind of food
that had thrilled her as a student in France. Utterly
original, Chez Panisse served fresh, local, simple, and
astonishingly delicious food. As America adopted
the destructive values of "fast food," her restaurant
became the beacon for the benefits of slow food. Now
her Edible Schoolyard movement is revolutionizing
school lunches as children plant, harvest, prepare,
and eat lunch, learning their place in the cycle of life.*

alice waters was born during World War II on April 28, 1944, in Chatham, New Jersey. Her father grew vegetables in a home Victory Garden to support the war effort. Alice remembers being dressed as queen of the garden in a skirt made of lettuce, a bracelet of radishes, a pepper anklet, a strawberry necklace, and an asparagus crown. She was a tiny, angelic-looking child with clear blue eyes and a fair complexion. She took in the tastes and smells of the world around her with especially keen senses. She loved her mother's pies and hated her dry brown health bread.

Her father's career in insurance took the family to Indiana and then to California, where Alice went to high school. Her friends were the brainy ones. But she chose to enter the University of California at Santa Barbara, known as a party school. While she loved parties, she and a friend transferred to the more serious campus at Berkeley.

the world split open

Then the turbulent 1960s began. The Civil Rights Movement was underway in the South, as people tried to persuade the government to pass laws granting true equality to African Americans. It looked as if the Vietnam War was going to suck the United States into what some saw as an immoral and endless conflict. Students were protesting against what the government was doing. But Berkeley had strict rules forbidding political activities on campus. In response, students formed a free-speech movement, held rallies and sit-ins, and eventually occupied one of the academic buildings. Alice felt that the world as she had known it had cracked open. Rules were being broken; there was a sense that young people could do anything, even change the world. It was an exciting and hopeful time. Waters threw herself into politics for a while, even helping manage a friend's campaign for office.

But then the upheaval became oppressive. She felt she had to escape it. Because she wanted to learn French, she applied to take her junior year in Paris. There, her first spoonful of soup was so delicious it made her think she had never eaten before—a brothy root-vegetable soup with lots of parsley and garlic, she recalls. Every day brought marvelous new tastes: apricot jam on a baguette, juicy peaches, rich pâté, a simple chicken with startling flavor.

Little restaurants were so affordable, she could try a different one every day. The cooks created menus based on the fresh ingredients bought from markets a few steps away. People took their time over meals, engaging in rich conversations. It was a different way of living. Alice loved everything her senses took in: the food served just so in rooms arranged down to the last detail, the smells, the sensation of each morsel in her mouth, even the dresses and hats French women wore. It was all magical to her, life as art.

a persistent idea

But the year came to an end. Back in Berkeley, Alice wanted to cook food in the French way and share her discoveries with her friends. She missed France painfully. Then, in 1968, a year after she graduated, Martin Luther King Jr. and Robert F. Kennedy were both gunned down. Along with much of the country, Alice was in despair. She couldn't bear more politics. She wanted to do something meaningful, but pleasurable.

Why not open a restaurant in Berkeley? She knew she could do it. And many of her friends were eager to help. First, she waited tables at a restaurant and found she was a much better cook than the chef there. She wrote a food column about flavor, trying out some of her ideas. Great food had to be made from great ingredients, at their peak of flavor.

Starting a restaurant took a lot of money. She wasn't quite ready. Her plan needed another ingredient. It came in the form of the Montessori method. She started as an assistant at a local Montessori school and loved it so much a friend suggested she go to London to be certified as a Montessori teacher.

the montessori method

The Montessori Method was developed by Maria Montessori (1870–1952), an Italian doctor who studied how children learn. In the schools she directed, children were encouraged to take in the world through their senses—seeing, hearing, smelling, tasting, feeling—and to work in multi-age groups in beautifully designed, pleasing settings. Guided by trained teachers, children tried out new skills until they mastered them. The special materials Maria created to facilitate learning are still used in Montessori schools around the world.

Waters loved the method, in which "the hands are the instrument of the mind," as founder Maria Montessori said. Children didn't sit at desks with workbooks but experimented, given clear instructions. During breaks in the certification classes, Waters traveled to Turkey and Greece. The bounty of delicious foods and the warm hospitality she found thrilled her, as they had in France. She would teach, but she was also even more determined to create a place for food and friendship.

creating chez panisse

Back in California, she taught in a Montessori school. Meanwhile, that passion for good food flowered. Waters sampled restaurants, refining her ideas about how to create her own. After persuading investors to fund her enterprise, she and some friends found an old house in Berkeley and furnished it with pleasingly mismatched tables and chairs. Every detail had to be just right: the lighting, the direction of the breezes from the nearby bay, and of course the menus. The food would be cooked by her friends and by people she liked when they applied for the job. But Alice understood from her Montessori training that it was important for everyone on the team to know how to do every phase of the work. When the restaurant was open, Alice would not be in the kitchen. She'd be in the dining room, greeting diners and overseeing service.

The all-important ingredients were hard to find in 1971, the year the restaurant opened. Few farmers were raising organic vegetables, for example. But San Francisco had ethnic markets—Japanese and Chinese, among them— that provided Alice with what she needed to begin. She wanted to surprise her patrons. She hired a forager who knew how to find wild edible foods that no other restaurant was serving.

Waters named the restaurant Chez Panisse. A friend had introduced her to the films of Marcel Pagnol set in a homey bar in Marseille, France. The characters charmed her: Fanny, the innocent young girl, and especially Panisse, the kindly older man who rescues her. His was the spirit she wanted to celebrate. Alice Waters gave no thought to making money from her restaurant. She wanted to make people love the taste of her food and to want to taste it again.

Chez Panisse had a rocky start. At first, the kitchen was chaos. Alice spent extravagantly to get the ingredients she wanted, and the restaurant lost money. Finally, Waters's father stepped in and began running it like a business. Her parents even mortgaged their home to pay off some debt.

It was worth the effort and sacrifice. People loved the food. Critics called Chez Panisse the best restaurant in California. Eventually it would be named the best restaurant in the United States. California cuisine, invented by Alice Waters, became as important as French cuisine. Many of the cooks who began at Chez Panisse opened their own restaurants in other places. What began so modestly became a movement for good, local, carefully and simply prepared meals.

Alice Waters's passion for delicious food never let her rest. She kept trying to improve the restaurant. She'd found farmers who could supply superb crops, but she needed more. So Chez Panisse bought its own farm.

food fast and slow

By the 1980s, life had speeded up for Americans. Fast-food chains multiplied. Food was raised or grown in factory conditions, with no concern for sustainability, and was available at all hours. But the little restaurant that offered one meal a day made from fresh, local ingredients was changing Americans' ideas about what they ate. Farmers markets, many with organic produce, began springing up. Home cooks discovered mesclun greens, first served at Chez Panisse, and many other ingredients never available before.

To Alice Waters, eating is a profound ritual, connecting us to nature and to each other. But while Chez Panisse was helping support a network of farmers, others were going out of business, their land sold to developers. How, Waters wondered, could she help to fight this powerful trend? She was still the activist who had rallied for free speech in the 1960s. One answer was to publish books with her ideas and with recipes from Chez Panisse, starting with *Chez Panisse Menu Cookbook* in 1982. The cookbooks became classics, won awards, and helped to spread her beliefs about food.

the edible schoolyard

Alice Waters and her husband, Stephen Singer, had one daughter, Fanny, born in 1983. (That marriage ended in 1997.) Having a child made Waters worry even more about America's food stock and the pesticides and herbicides in food production. She also worried about the kinds of foods so many Americans were eating, what children were learning about food, and the fact that families had no time to eat together and talk.

Every day she passed the Martin Luther King Jr. Middle School in Berkeley on her way from home to the restaurant. It was covered with graffiti and looked deserted. The entire yard was blacktop. The children bought microwaved lunches every day from a snack bar. After she mentioned her dismay at the school's appearance on a radio show in 1994, the principal reached out to Waters. He gave her a tour and she gave him an idea: turn the schoolyard into a giant garden where the children could grow their own lunches. And the lunches would be free.

It took six months for the principal to come around, but he finally did. Waters insisted the whole yard be a garden—her proposal was all or nothing.

He agreed, and the staff and volunteers tore up the blacktop and planted the first crop of the Edible Schoolyard. Children in the program learn where food comes from by planting, cultivating, harvesting, preparing, serving, and sharing it. As they compare tastes and quality, they learn table manners, cooperation, and judgment. It's learning through the senses, the Montessori way. Today, all the Berkeley public schools and some fifty-five hundred others around the country are part of the Edible Schoolyard program.

beyond the schoolyard

When her daughter went to college at Yale University, Waters established the Yale Sustainable Food Project. She transformed the food service at the American Academy in Rome. She has partnered with the Slow Food Movement that began in Italy and now inspires people worldwide.

Alice Waters ignited a revolution with the help of her many friends. Now she is leading a crusade. She is a deceptively gentle persuader who has, her friends say, an iron will. "Of course it's possible," she will say about a difficult proposal. To her, good food and all the goodness that surrounds it should define our way of life. She quotes the great French food writer Jean Anthelme Brillat-Savarin (1755–1826): "The destiny of nations depends on the manner in which they feed themselves."

Alice Waters is pointing us toward a better destiny.

"Good food is a right, not a privilege."

—alice waters

TEMPLE GRANDIN

*scientist who changed
perceptions of autism*

1947–

For most of the twentieth century, autism—a condition that impairs the ability to communicate and interact—was misunderstood and hidden away. Much of the attention on helping children and adults on the autism spectrum lead fulfilling lives is thanks to Temple Grandin, who has given us the inside story of what it is like to be autistic. Her great success as an animal scientist in making slaughterhouses and feedlots more humane is an inspiration to children on the spectrum. To young people with autism, she urges: Become really good at something, persevere with it, and seize opportunities when they come along. "The world," says Grandin, "needs all kinds of minds."

temple grandin's

early childhood was marked by frustration and fear. Born on August 29, 1947, in Boston, Massachusetts, she didn't speak until she was three and a half. People assumed she was deaf. She sat for hours sifting sand through her fingers. While she longed for the calm that hugging brought, she hated being hugged because it overwhelmed her. Unable to communicate, she would rock back and forth with a blank expression. It wasn't clear what was wrong.

There were horrific meltdowns, too. "One minute I was fine, the next minute I was on the floor, kicking and screaming like a crazed wildcat," Temple recalled. "I remember not wanting to wear a hat. So I screamed and threw it on the floor of the car, and Mother said, 'Put it back on.' So I screamed and chucked it out the window."

Temple's inability to communicate or process information and her extreme sensitivity to light, sound, and touch are symptoms of autism.

autism spectrum disorder

Autism is also called "autism spectrum disorder." A *spectrum* refers to a continuous range of something—think of a rainbow. There are many different types of autism, which is why it is appropriate to refer to the autism spectrum. Its conditions include experiencing challenges and delays with communication, being sensitive to sensory input, repeating behaviors, and having difficulty interacting with others.

About one in sixty-eight children in the United States are on the autism spectrum. People on the so-called "high functioning" end of the spectrum have been described as having Asperger's syndrome. Compared with others on the spectrum, people with Asperger's don't have significant delays in language development and learning.

the diagnosis

Finally, when Temple was three, doctors diagnosed autism. Back then, the condition wasn't understood. The medical experts believed Temple was brain-damaged and should be put in an institution. Her mother refused to do that.

At the time, mothers were often blamed for their children's autism. Temple's mother, though, refused to believe it was something she had caused. She never gave up on helping her daughter adjust to the condition, no matter how extreme Temple's symptoms were.

Her mother read books to Temple every day, giving her a love of literature and a way to understand the world. She found a caregiver and private schools, which the family was fortunate to be able to afford. Temple was taught how to live by the rules of the world. If she pulled something off a shelf in a store, she was told not to do that. Before long, her parents could take her to restaurants, confident she would exhibit good manners. Temple now calls it being "molded and shaped" so she could enter society.

understanding autism

Autism has only recently been studied and understood. Russian psychologist Grunya Sukhareva first identified its behaviors in the 1920s. Hans Asperger treated children he called "autistic" in 1940s Vienna. At the same time, Leo Kanner began studying autistic children in the United States. Kanner realized that autism was a distinct syndrome, with a group of identifying behaviors. For years he blamed the condition on emotionally cold parents but later concluded that children were born with the condition.

The research and publications of Swiss American scientist Isabelle Rapin went further. She helped debunk the myth that a mother's poor parenting caused the condition. She also promoted early education for autistic children and used the term *autism spectrum disorder*, first proposed by a British doctor, Lorna Wing.

Temple's parents sent her to school as well. There, she was fortunate to have a writing teacher who insisted that she rewrite her school essays until they were graceful and accurate. That gave her the foundation to become a writer. A science teacher, William Carlock, became a mentor when he realized Temple learned by visualizing—thinking in pictures, not words. He told her that would be an advantage in conducting science projects. She discovered that she had the ability to draw things and then build them. When still very young, she constructed kites and helicopters, and when they failed, she improved her designs until they succeeded. She learned from failure, and she developed a work ethic that has made her extraordinarily productive.

But in high school her schoolmates labeled her a "weirdo," and she had to put up with merciless bullying. Panic attacks sent her to her room, where she wrapped herself in blankets.

the squeeze chute

Then, when she was fourteen, her mother remarried and Temple's life was transformed. Her stepfather's sister owned a ranch in Arizona. Temple's mother sent her there for the summer.

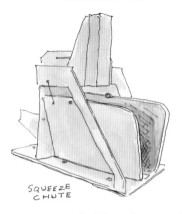

SQUEEZE
CHUTE

It was a time of momentous discoveries for her. Temple watched the animals on the ranch and realized that both she and they used visual clues and memory to navigate the world. She shrank from human touch. So did they. It made her think she could instinctively understand animal behavior.

One day, watching a line of cattle being herded along to be vaccinated, Temple noticed the squeeze chute—a stall used to hold each animal still. She couldn't get it out of her mind. Could a contraption like that stop her horrendous panic attacks? Her aunt allowed her to get into the chute herself. The effect was miraculous. She felt calm. It was like being hugged, but better because she was in control of the hug.

When Temple got home, she built her own squeeze chute in her bedroom. It was lined with foam and worked with compressed air. The pressure never failed to calm her down and ease the effects of nervous stimulation. A psychiatrist who was treating Temple disapproved of the chute and tried to cure her of her "fixation" on it. Fortunately, he failed. Her wonderful Mr. Carlock told her if she wanted to defeat the opponents of the machine, she should research why it worked. It was a lesson in the practical application of science on life situations.

At Franklin Pierce College (now University), she got more encouragement. When she failed a biology quiz, the professor tutored her after class instead of letting her flunk out. She resolved to study hard and graduated second in her class in 1970. She was on her way to becoming a scientist, with a specialty in animal behavior. She went on to earn a master's degree and then a PhD in animal science.

designing humane methods

In the 1970s, the field of animal behavior was exclusively male. She tried to conduct research into feedlots, where cattle were fed, but men objected, saying they couldn't believe a woman knew anything about the subject. She was told, "Cowboys' wives don't want you here. You can't be here." When she was kicked out of a feedlot altogether, she retaliated, as she later put it, by getting a press pass and writing a column for a cattlemen's magazine.

She began using her drawing and engineering talents to design animal-handling equipment for companies, especially slaughterhouses. The company she founded—which is still going strong—is called Grandin Livestock Handling Systems, Inc.

The procedure she focused on was humane slaughtering of cattle. Among her clients was the McDonald's Corporation. The company hired Grandin in 1999 to design an improved system. By then, she was a known expert in the field, and she helped the company improve conditions so the process was less stressful to cattle.

She saw details in the world around her that other people didn't see. Animals, she understood, also operated visually, taking cues from their environment. In ordinary slaughterhouses, cattle could see what lay ahead as they approached their deaths and became fearful and agitated. Grandin designed a plain, curved (because cattle like to move in circles), comforting chute with no visual distractions.

She also stopped the practice of leading cattle from bright sunlight into dark areas, which upset them. They recoiled from the color yellow and from clanking noises, so these were eliminated. The quality of the meat improved dramatically because glycogen, produced in the animal's flesh by stress, was greatly reduced. Today, more than half the cattle in the United States are slaughtered by her method. Grandin had similar results with her work for the pork industry.

Her 2005 book, *Animals in Translation: Using the Mysteries of Autism to Decode Animal Behavior*, has been very influential in persuading the industry and ordinary people to approach animals on their terms. She says of the animals we eat, "We owe them a decent life and a decent death."

decoding autism from the inside

While animal behavior has been Grandin's profession, autism is at the core of her identity. She has made it a mission to explain the condition, both scientifically and emotionally, in books, lectures, and films. She gives advice to parents and children alike, stressing the talent rather than the limitation in autism.

Instead of trying to stop fixations in autistic children, Grandin recommends using them to their benefit. If a child is fixated on trains, insert trains into lessons about other things. Another suggestion is to learn from the child's behavior. If a child starts screaming in a big store, it is probably because the fluorescent lights are flickering, a sensory torture for them.

Grandin is distressed that manners and good behavior are not taught as much as when she was young. People living with autism would benefit from those lessons. (So would all children.) And schools should consider practical-skills programs, like shop class, which many autistic children are good at.

Her advice for high-functioning teens with Asperger's syndrome would be liberating for many young people, whether on the spectrum or not. "I really believe there's a certain portion of high-functioning Asperger's patients who need to be going to the university and getting in with their intellectual peers, and just skipping the whole teenage mess!"

Grandin thinks Einstein was a high-functioning autistic person who lived in a time that was more open to different kinds of brains. "How," she asks, "could a patent clerk, as Einstein was at the time he wrote it, get a groundbreaking paper published in a physics journal in 2005? I just don't think it would happen. An Einstein today would end up driving the FedEx truck or something, rather than concentrating on his theories."

"Parents get so worried about the deficits that they don't build up the strengths, but those skills could turn into a job," said Grandin, who addresses scientific advances in understanding autism in her newest book, *The Autistic Brain: Thinking Across the Spectrum*. "These kids often have uneven skills. We need to be a lot more flexible about things. Don't hold these math geniuses back. You're going to have to give them special ed in reading because that tends to be the pattern, but let them go ahead in math."

Temple Grandin's career is an inspiration. She is currently a professor of animal science at Colorado State University and has published more than a dozen books and hundreds of scholarly articles. She lectures all over the world, consults for meat-processing plants, and in 2016, was inducted into the American Academy of Arts and Sciences.

Her heroic career is still in high gear. Using her extraordinary insights and ability to communicate colorfully and forcefully, she has enlightened humanity about both the animal mind and the autistic mind.

"Autism is an important part of who I am. I like the logical way I think and I wouldn't want to change that, but my principal identity is being a scientist."

—temple grandin

SECOND WAVE FEMINISM

sisterhood becomes powerful

early 1960s–1970s

While individuals—like the twenty-one women featured in this book—can give voice to movements for change, a revolution happens when many people join in a common cause. That was the case with the First Wave of feminism, as the suffrage movement in the late 1800s and early 1900s was known. It was also true of the Second Wave, or the women's liberation movement, in the 1960s and '70s. The Second Wave profoundly changed the way women think about themselves and the way men think about women. A few individuals became more famous than others, but the movement was a collective with no designated leaders. Feminists in the Second Wave—many from the Civil Rights and anti–Vietnam War Movements—believed in gender equality. The changes these revolutions brought to American culture and politics are with us still. That women are still being harassed by men today shows that the fight for equality goes on.

after the suffrage movement led to women's right

to vote in 1920, feminism lost momentum. By the 1950s, with few exceptions, if you were a young woman and attended college, you were being educated to raise superior children.

In your future family, your husband would be boss. If you needed to work, you consulted want ads listing jobs based on gender. The women's list included secretary, Gal Friday (a general assistant), clerk, and nurse. For your interview, you wore a hat, gloves, heels, a dress, and underneath, a girdle, garter belt, and stockings.

a man's world

If you worked, you earned far less than any man did in his first job. If you tried to advance, you were called "unfeminine." There was no term for "sexual harassment"—and little you could do about it. You were responsible for the reactions of boys and men. If a boss or a date "went too far," people believed it was probably your fault. You could not legally rent a place to live, take out a loan from a bank, or get a credit card without a man to cosign for you. You would be refused service at many bars and restaurants if you went alone. You couldn't sit on a jury in several states.

You would marry if a man proposed, and after that your identity was "wife" or "Mrs." If your husband had a good job, you might have lived in one of the suburbs that sprang up after World War II. He went off to work and you stayed busy with housework and children and made him his dinner. Being a female meant you were limited in what you could do and how important you were. And most females, having grown up with that limitation, accepted it.

Then atomic testing during the Cold War with the Soviet Union introduced radioactivity in the milk American children drank. Outraged mothers started Women Strike for Peace to protest above-ground testing. The protest helped push the United States and the Soviet Union into signing a nuclear test–ban treaty in 1963. Women saw that organizing around an issue had the potential to bring change.

the first stirrings and now

Also in 1963, Betty Friedan published *The Feminine Mystique*, which described the isolation and despair felt by many educated women housebound in suburbs. Women everywhere were stunned to recognize themselves in her book. In the South, Freedom Summer attracted young people who tried to register African Americans to vote. Two of the volunteers were Casey Hayden and Mary King. They were reading another shocking book, *The Second Sex* by Simone de Beauvoir. It awakened them to the second-class status that they endured as women. Hayden and King wrote a 1965 memo describing their experience of sexism in the Civil Rights Movement. It was read by young women activists around the country.

Women were looking at themselves and the way they were treated. Many were very disturbed and ready to object.

the second sex

Published in 1949, *The Second Sex* helped launch the Second Wave. Author Simone de Beauvoir, a French philosopher, made the argument for feminism on philosophical, emotional, and historical grounds. Historically, she wrote, women are seen only in relation to men: "Humanity is male and man defines woman not in herself but as relative to him." In her native France and in the United States, the book was read by intellectuals and college students and slowly touched larger and larger numbers of women.

In 1966, Betty Friedan and more than two dozen others founded NOW, the National Organization for Women, saying that women should not have to choose between family and meaningful work. They declared the problems of women were problems for everyone. NOW drew up a bill of rights for women, asking for maternity leave, day care centers for working women's children, income tax deductions for childcare costs, the right to reproductive freedom, and equality in areas including education and employment.

Around the country, younger women, many of them in the Civil Rights and anti–Vietnam War Movements, started informal groups with more radical demands and less polite methods. One faction carried a blond dummy representing Traditional Womanhood to a 1968 anti-war rally in Washington, DC, and announced they would bury it. Others marched with banners declaring SISTERHOOD IS POWERFUL, which became a rallying cry for women everywhere.

"The personal is political" was another mantra. Women who had been talking about *male chauvinism* (an attitude of superiority toward women) began using the word *sexism*, and the term stuck.

raised consciousness

New York Radical Women, a small group of feminists, held "consciousness-raising" sessions, sharing life experiences demeaning to women. Speaking honestly about themselves and listening to each other, they came to understand they had been held back because they were women. It was, for most, a thrilling and liberating revelation.

The poet Muriel Rukeyser asked, "What would happen if one woman told the truth about her life? The world would split open." That was the intent of consciousness-raising: split the world open, expose the unfairness to girls and women. Consciousness-raising proved to be one of the most powerful tools ever devised for making social change.

This mass awakening to the fact that women were all second-class citizens inspired them not just to work to level the playing field but to analyze everything about being the "second sex." Having once assumed they had to shape themselves to fit into the man's world, women realized it was the world that had to change to fit them, and they protested sexism wherever they saw it.

The Miss America Pageant in Atlantic City was a prime example, featuring women as objects, wearing swimsuits and judged in the most superficial way. A group of radical women from New York staged their own mock pageant, crowning a sheep "queen" and tossing "instruments of torture" such as hair curlers and bras into a Freedom Trash Can. The *New York Times* reported that women protesting the pageant had burned their bras in Atlantic City—they had not—and "bra burners" became shorthand for the activists.

It was a watershed moment. TV crews broadcast the story, and the publicity made Women's Lib hot news. That didn't mean the media took it seriously. But things were changing. Everyone had to decide where she—and he—stood.

Women protested sexism in medical care as well, taking charge of their own health. Many doctors had long treated their female patients like children. A group of Boston women researched every aspect of women's bodies and published *Our Bodies, Ourselves*, a handbook that became a runaway success. "Natural childbirth," with no medication, became popular as women realized a coach and a midwife could usually provide all the help they needed. In New York, the radical Redstockings disrupted a legislative hearing on abortion, which was still illegal, demanding repeal of the laws.

And women protested the way they were depicted in the media. In 1970, feminists invaded the office of the male editor of *Ladies' Home Journal* and held him prisoner. Meanwhile, feminists started to produce their own magazines and books—more than five hundred new publications—between 1968 and 1973. The Feminist Press was founded. Gloria Steinem and Dorothy Pitman Hughes launched *Ms.* magazine to be a megaphone for feminism. Men predicted it would fail. Instead, women all over the country read it with passionate interest.

The Second Wave was driven by women from every part of society, every age, every color and ethnicity. Women made themselves experts on issues, protested, and ran for office. Shirley Chisholm had been in Congress since 1968. In 1971, Bella Abzug joined her. There was the sense that equality was coming at last. "To be a feminist in the early 1970s—bliss it was in that dawn, to be alive. Not an I-love-you . . . could touch it. We lived then, all of us, inside the . . . embrace of feminism: There was no other place to be except with each other," said writer Vivian Gornick. She and her feminist sisters wondered: How could this movement be stopped?

struggling for equal rights

In 1970, as part of a "strike for Equality," some fifty thousand women marched in New York City to celebrate the fiftieth anniversary of the Nineteenth Amendment, which granted women the right to vote. A daring group hung a giant banner on the Statue of Liberty: WOMEN OF THE WORLD UNITE. In forty-two states, women went on strike from their jobs (and from cooking and cleaning at home) to support equality in employment, education, and other areas.

But change would not come easily. In 1971, President Richard Nixon vetoed a bill that would have provided two billion dollars for national childcare, arguing that it threatened family life. No similar bill has come close to passing since then.

In 1972, Congress passed the Equal Rights Amendment, first proposed by Jeannette Rankin (the first woman elected to Congress) in 1922. It would make equal rights for women part of the US Constitution. For the ERA to become law, three-quarters of the states would have to ratify—give it formal approval.

Title IX, requiring gender equality in education, including athletic programs, became law the same year. Women's sports could finally come into their own.

Shirley Chisholm ran for president. The National Women's Political Caucus, founded by Chisholm, Steinem, Friedan, Abzug, and others, worked to increase women's participation in "all areas of political and public life—as elected and appointed officials, as delegates to national party conventions, as judges . . . and as lobbyists, voters, and campaign organizers."

Not everyone was for women's liberation. The opposition found a champion in Phyllis Schlafly, a lawyer, housewife, and mother of six children. She launched her campaign against the Equal Rights Amendment, claiming that feminists "hate men, marriage, and children."

Women's groups realized that they had been infiltrated by agents of the FBI, which considered them dangerous. It was infuriating, but it also added to the excitement.

progress and decline

In 1973, the Supreme Court's *Roe v. Wade* decision affirmed a woman's right to abortion. The Court's opinion quoted an earlier case that had "recognized the right of the individual, married or single, to be free from unwarranted governmental intrusion into matters so fundamentally affecting a person as the decision whether to bear . . . a child." The backlash was powerful. The nation was (and still is) divided in its opinion. In 1975, the National Right to Life PAC, a committee to fund lobbying of Congress to reverse *Roe v. Wade*, was formed.

In 1974, Congress passed a law giving women the right to borrow money from a bank. Some one thousand colleges were offering courses in women's studies, recovering forgotten and suppressed history. Little League admitted girls to baseball teams. National women's football and basketball leagues were founded. Many men took on more housework and childcare (although far less than women's share). More and more women became doctors, lawyers, and engineers, though women—especially women of color—were still a small minority in these fields, and were not represented in the top levels.

At the first National Women's Conference, twenty thousand women in

Houston endorsed a National Plan of Action. Across town, Phyllis Schlafly held her own counter-rally, opposing the ERA and launching a campaign to stop it. The amendment has yet to be ratified.

During the 1970s, the Supreme Court had struck down laws that discriminated against women, but many more remained. Meanwhile, society was changing; there was more violence, more divorce, more poverty, all making people more conservative and attached to traditional roles for women and men.

By 1980, the Second Wave was coming to an end. The Republican Party, which had supported the ERA and abortion rights, began to oppose them both. But the birth control pill and *Roe v. Wade* had profoundly altered the status of women, giving them control of their unique ability to reproduce. More women were graduating from law, medical, and engineering schools. They were competing in school and professional sports. Many more people were conscious of sexism in the media and society. The Second Wave had made women's rights human rights. A generation had awakened and fought for those rights. But sexism is ancient and persistent and must be beaten back again and again.

eight things a woman couldn't do before the second wave

1. Be legally guaranteed the right to get a credit card

2. Take out a bank loan

3. Be legally guaranteed job protection as a pregnant woman

4. Report cases of sexual harassment at school or work

5. Exercise reproductive choice in most states

6. Serve on a jury in most states

7. Get a divorce easily

8. Use her maiden name if she were married

sources

JANE ADDAMS: CHAMPION OF IMMIGRANTS AND THE POOR

Addams, Jane. *Peace and Bread in Time of War*. New York: The Macmillan Co., 1922. Reprint, New York: J. S. Ozer, 1972.

———. *Twenty Years at Hull House*. New York: The Macmillan Co., 1910. Reprint, Urbana: University of Illinois Press, 1990.

Almgren, Gunnar and Taryn Lindhorst. *The Safety-Net Health Care System: Health Care at the Margins*. New York: Springer Publishing Co., 2011.

Brown, Victoria B. *The Education of Jane Addams*. Philadelphia: University of Pennsylvania Press, 2004.

Jane Addams Hull-House Museum. https://www.hullhousemuseum.org/

Knight, Louise W. *Citizen: Jane Addams and the Struggle for Democracy*. Chicago: University of Chicago Press, 2005.

———. *Jane Addams: Spirit in Action*. New York: W. W. Norton & Co., 2010.

ETHEL PERCY ANDRUS: CHANGING THE FACE OF AGING

"A Chicken Coop: The Unlikely Birthplace of AARP." AARP publication, n.d. https://states .aarp.org/chicken-coop-unlikely-birthplace-aarp

Crippen, Dorothy et al., ed. *Power of Years: The Wisdom of Ethel Percy Andrus*. Long Beach, CA: NRTA & AARP, 1968.

Kiger, Patrick J. "Champions of Aging: Ethel Percy Andrus." AARP.org. https://www.aarp.org /politics-society/history/champions-of-aging-photos/ethel-percy-andrus-aarp-founder/

"The Life of Ethel Percy Andrus in Her Own Words." AARP publication, n.d.

Walker, Craig. "Ethel Andrus: How One Woman Changed America." Speech delivered at Ojai Valley Museum, 1 May 2011. http://ojaihistory.com/ethel-percy-andrus-how-one-woman -changed-america/

ELLA BAKER: GODMOTHER OF THE CIVIL RIGHTS MOVEMENT

"Baker, Ella Josephine." Zinn Education Project. zinnedproject.org/materials/baker-ella/

"Ella Baker." SNCC Digital Gateway, snccdigital.org/people/ella-baker/

Grant, Joanne. *Ella Baker: Freedom Bound*. New York: John Wiley & Sons, 1998.

———. director. *Fundi: The Story of Ella Baker*. Icarus Films, 1981.

Ransby, Barbara. *Ella Baker and the Black Freedom Movement*. Chapel Hill, NC: The University of North Carolina Press, 2003.

GERTRUDE BERG: WRITER, PRODUCER, STAR

Berg, Gertrude. *Molly and Me*. New York: McGraw-Hill, 1961.

Foreman, Joel, ed. *The Other Fifties: Interrogating Midcentury American Icons*. Urbana, IL: University of Illinois Press, 1997.

Newcomb, Horace, ed. *Encyclopedia of Television, Vol. 3*. London: Fitzroy Dearborn Publishers, 2004.

Smith, Glenn D. *"Something on My Own": Gertrude Berg and American Broadcasting, 1929–1956*. Syracuse, NY: Syracuse University Press, 2007.

RACHEL CARSON: DEFENDER OF THE ENVIRONMENT

Carson, Rachel. *The Sea Around Us*. New York: Oxford University Press, 1950. Reissued by Oxford University Press in 1989 with a new introduction by Ann W. Zwinger and an afterword by Jeffrey S. Levinton.

———. *Silent Spring*. New York: Houghton Mifflin Co., 1962. Fiftieth anniversary edition reissued by Houghton Mifflin Co. in 2002 with a new introduction by Linda Lear and an afterword by Edward O. Wilson.

Dunn, J. R. "Rachel Carson and the Deaths of Millions," American Thinker, 25 May 2007. https://www.americanthinker.com/articles/2007/05/rachel_carson_and_the_deaths_o.html

Griswold, Eliza. "How 'Silent Spring' Ignited the Environmental Movement," *New York Times*, 21 September 2012. www.nytimes.com/2012/09/23/magazine/how-silent-spring-ignited-the-environmental-movement.html

Lear, Linda. *Rachel Carson: Witness for Nature*. New York: Mariner Books, 2009.

———. "Rachel Carson's Silence." The *Pittsburgh Post-Gazette*, April 13, 2014.

Lewis, Jack. "The Birth of EPA." EPA Journal, November 1985. https://archive.epa.gov/epa/aboutepa/birth-epa.html

Lytle, Mark H. *The Gentle Subversive: Rachel Carson, Silent Spring, and the Rise of the Environmental Movement*. New York: Oxford University Press, 2007.

Popkin, Gabriel. "Right Fish, Wrong Pond." Johns Hopkins Magazine (Summer 2013). https://hub.jhu.edu/magazine/2013/summer/rachel-carson-at-hopkins/

"Rachel Carson" (documentary). PBS: American Experience, Jan. 24, 2017. https://www.pbs.org/wgbh/americanexperience/films/rachel-carson/

"Rachel Carson's Biography," rachelcarson.org

Stein, Karen F. *Rachel Carson: Challenging Authors*. Rotterdam, The Netherlands: Sense Publishers, 2012.

SHIRLEY CHISHOLM: POLITICAL TRAILBLAZER

Chisholm, Shirley. *The Good Fight*. New York: Harper & Row, 1973.

————. "I'd Rather be Black than Female." https://www.scribd.com/document/170718971/10
-Chisholm-id-Rather-Be-Black-Than-Female

Foner, Nancy, ed. *Islands in the City: West Indian Migration to New York*. Berkeley, CA:
University of California Press, 2001.

"The Greensboro Sit-In" (article), History.com.https://www.history.com/topics/black-history
/the-greensboro-sit-in

Gutgold, Nichola D. *Still Paving the Way for Madam President*. Lanham, MD: Lexington Books, 2017.

"Ku Klux Klan." Southern Poverty Law Center. https://www.splcenter.org/fighting-hate
/extremist-files/ideology/ku-klux-klan

Landers, Jackson. "'Unbought and Unbossed': When a Black Woman Ran for the White
House." Smithsonianmag.com, 25 April 2016. www.smithsonianmag.com/smithsonian
-institution/unbought-and-unbossed-when-black woman-ran-for-the-white
-house-180958699/

"Remarks by the President at Medal of Freedom Ceremony." Obama White House Archives,
24 November 2015. https://obamawhitehouse.archives.gov/the-press-office/2015/11/24
/remarks-president-medal-freedom-ceremony

Winslow, Barbara. *Shirley Chisholm: Catalyst for Change*. Boulder, CO: Westview Press, 2014.

JOAN GANZ COONEY: INNOVATOR OF EDUCATIONAL TV

Carilli, Theresa and Jane Campbell, eds. *Women and the Media: Diverse Perspectives*. Lanham,
MD: UPA, 2005.

Dominus, Susan. "A Girly-Girl Joins the 'Sesame' Boys." The *New York Times*, 6 Aug. 2006.
http://www.nytimes.com/2006/08/06/arts/television/06domi.html

"Joan Ganz Cooney." Archive of American Television. www.emmytvlegends.org/interviews
/people/joan-ganz-cooney

"Joan Ganz Cooney." *PBS: Who Made America?* https://www.pbs.org/wgbh/theymadeamerica
/whomade/cooney_hi.html

"Makers: Joan Ganz Cooney: How Big Bird Was Born" (video), 6 June 2013. Makers.com.
https://www.makers.com/joan-ganz-cooney

O'Dell, Cary. *Women Pioneers in Television: Biographies of Fifteen Industry Leaders*. Jefferson,
NC: McFarland Co., 1997.

Season 47, sesameworkshop.org. www.sesameworkshop.org/season47/news/see-amazing-in
-all-children-press-release/

ISADORA DUNCAN: FOUNDER OF MODERN DANCE

Daly, Ann. *Done Into Dance: Isadora Duncan in America*. Bloomington, IN: 1995. Reprint: Middletown, CT: Wesleyan University Press, 2002.

Duncan, Doree et al., ed. *Life into Art: Isadora Duncan and Her World*. New York: W. W. Norton & Co., 1993.

Duncan, Isadora. *My Life*. New York: Boni & Liveright, Inc., 1927.

Landing, Kristie. "Isadora Duncan: A Revolutionary Dancer." National Museum of Women in the Arts. https://nmwa.org/blog/2012/06/15/isadora-duncan-a-revolutionary-dancer/

Terry, Walter. *Isadora Duncan: Her Life, Her Art, Her Legacy*. New York: Dodd, Mead, 1984.

Wood, Ean. *Headlong Through Life: The Story of Isadora Duncan*. Leicester, England: Book Guild Ltd., 2006.

BARBARA GITTINGS: MOTHER OF THE GAY RIGHTS MOVEMENT

Baim, Tracy. *Barbara Gittings: Gay Pioneer*. Chicago, IL: Prairie Avenue Productions, 2015.

"Barbara Gittings." LGBTHistoryMonth.com. lgbthistorymonth.com/barbara-gittings?tab-biography

"Barbara Gittings." Philadelphia LGBT History Project, Outhistory.org, 2 February 1993. outhistory.org/exhibits/show/philadelphia-lgbt-interviews/interviews/barbara-gittings

"Barbara Gittings." PBS: Out of the Past. https://www.pbs.org/outofthepast/past/p5/gittings.html

Collins, Gail. *When Everything Changed: The Amazing Journey of American Women from 1960 to the Present*. Boston: Little, Brown and Co., 2009.

Fox, Margalit. "Barbara Gittings, 74, Prominent Gay Rights Activist Since '50s, Dies." *New York Times*, 15 March 2007. https://www.nytimes.com/2007/03/15/obituaries/15gittings.html

Gallo, Marcia M. *Different Daughters: A History of the Daughters of Bilitis and the Rise of the Lesbian Rights Movement*. Emeryville, CA: Seal Press, 2006.

Mixner, David and Dennis Bailey. *Brave Journeys: Profiles in Gay and Lesbian Courage*. New York: Bantam Books, 2000.

TEMPLE GRANDIN: SCIENTIST WHO CHANGED PERCEPTIONS OF AUTISM

"Autism First-Hand: An Expert Interview with Temple Grandin, Ph.D." Medscape, 3 November 2017. www.medscape.org/viewarticle/498153

Autism Speaks. www.autismspeaks.org/

Jackson, Mick, director. *Temple Grandin*. HBO Films, 2010. https://www.hbo.com/movies/temple-grandin

Sacks, Oliver. *An Anthropologist on Mars: Seven Paradoxical Tales*. New York: Picador, 2012.

"Temple Grandin." Makers, www.makers.com/temple-grandin

"Temple Grandin: The Woman Who Talks to Animals." NPR, 5 February 2010. www.npr.org /templates/transcript/transcript.php?storyId=123383699

Temple Grandin's Official Autism Website. www.templegrandin.com/

GRACE MURRAY HOPPER: COMPUTER PROGRAMMING PIONEER

"Biography of Grace Murray Hopper." Office of the President, Yale University. https:// president.yale.edu/biography-grace-murray-hopper

Cushman, John H. "Admiral Hopper's Farewell." *New York Times*, 14 August 1986. https://www .nytimes.com/1986/08/14/us/washington-talk-admiral-hopper-s-farewell.html

"The Engines." Computer History Museum. www.computerhistory.org/babbage/engines/

Isaacson, Walter. "Grace Hopper, Computing Pioneer." *Harvard Gazette*, 3 December 2014. https://news.harvard.edu/gazette/story/2014/12/grace-hopper-computing-pioneer/

Williams, Kathleen Broome. *Grace Hopper: Admiral of the Cyber Sea*. Annapolis, MD: Naval Institute Press, 2012.

DOLORES HUERTA: THE LABOR ORGANIZER WHO SAID "YES, WE CAN!"

Bratt, Peter, director. *Dolores*. 5 Stick Films, 2017.www.doloresthemovie.com

"'Dolores' Focuses on Life of Labor and Civil Rights Leader Dolores Huerta." NPR, 22 January 2017. https://www.npr.org/2017/01/22/511103628/dolores-focuses-on-life-of-labor-and civil rights leader dolores huerta

"Dolores Huerta." Makers. www.makers.com/dolores-huerta

García, Mario T. *The Chicano Movement: Perspectives from the Twenty-First Century*. New York: Routledge, 2014.

———, ed. *A Dolores Huerta Reader*. Albuquerque, NM: University of New Mexico Press, 2008.

Godoy, Maria. "Dolores Huerta: The Civil Rights Icon Who Showed Farmworkers 'Sí Se Puede.'" NPR, 17 September 2017. www.npr.org/sections/thesalt/2017/09/17/551490281 /dolores-huerta-the-civil-rights-icon-who-showed-farmworkers-si-se-pued

La Botz, Dan. *Cesar Chavez and La Causa*. New York: Pearson Longman, 2005.

Vázquez, Francisco H. *Latino/a Thought: Culture, Politics, and Society*. Lanham, MD: Rowman & Littlefield Publishers, 2009.

BILLIE JEAN KING: CHAMPION FOR SPORTS AND EQUALITY

Baker, William Joseph. *Sports in the Western World*. Urbana and Chicago: University of Illinois Press, 1982.

Belzer, Jason. "The (R)evolution of Sports Sponsorships." *Forbes*, 22 April 2013. https://www.forbes.com/sites/jasonbelzer/2013/04/22/the-revolution-of-sports-sponsorship

Billie Jean King Leadership Initiative Website. http://www.bjkli.org/

Festle, Mary Jo. *Playing Nice: Politics and Apologies in Women's Sports*. New York: Columbia University Press, 1996.

Stanley, Alessandra. "The Legacy of Billie Jean King, an Athlete Who Demanded Equal Pay." *New York Times*, 26 April 2006. https://www.nytimes.com/2006/04/26/arts/television/the-legacy-of-billie-jean-king-an-athlete-who-demanded.html

Ware, Susan. *Game, Set, Match: Billie Jean King and the Revolution in Women's Sports*. Chapel Hill: University of North Carolina Press, 2011.

DOROTHEA LANGE: ELOQUENT EYE ON A HIDDEN AMERICA

"Dorothea Lange: 'Daring to Look.'" NPR, 20 July 2008. www.npr.org/templates/story/story.php?storyId=92656801

The Dust Bowl, Ken Burns, PBS. https://www.pbs.org/kenburns/dustbowl/bios/dorothea-lange

Gordon, Linda. *Dorothea Lange: A Life Beyond Limits*. New York: W. W. Norton and Co., 2009.

Lange, Dorothea, with introduction and commentary by Linda Gordon. *Dorothea Lange. Aperture Masters of Photography series*. New York: Aperture, 2014.

Meltzer, Milton. *Dorothea Lange: A Photographer's Life*. Syracuse, NY: Syracuse University Press, 2000.

Partridge, Elizabeth. *Restless Spirit: The Life and Work of Dorothea Lange*. New York: Puffin Books, 2001.

PATSY MINK: CHAMPION FOR WOMEN AND GIRLS IN EDUCATION

"40th Anniversary of Title IX." National Archives and Records Administration. www.obamawhitehouse.archives.gov/blog/2012/06/21/40th-anniversary-title-ix

"Gwendolyn Mink Oral History Interview," Office of the Historian, US House of Representatives, 14 March 2016. https://www.history.house.gov/Oral-History/Women/Women-Transcripts/mink-transcript

Mertens, Richard. "Political Pioneer: Patsy Mink, JD '51." *The University of Chicago Magazine*, Sept–Oct. 2012. https://mag.uchicago.edu/law-policy-society/political-pioneer

"Mink, Patsy Takemoto." U.S. House of Representatives: History, Art & Archives. https://history.house.gov/People/detail/18329

"A Modern Father of Our Constitution: An Interview with Former Senator Birch Bayh," Vol. 79. *Fordham Law Review* 781 (2011). https://ir.lawnet.fordham.edu/cgi/viewcontent.cgi?article=4689&context=flr

Title IX Resource Guide: U.S. Department of Education. Washington, DC: US Department of Education Office for Civil Rights, April 2015.

Winslow, Barbara. "The Impact of Title IX." The Gilder Lehrman Institute of American History, *History & Now 2* April 2012. https://www.gilderlehrman.org/history-by-era/seventies /essays/impact-title-ix

VERA RUBIN: QUEEN OF DARK MATTER

Alfred, Randy. "Dec. 30, 1924: Hubble Reveals We Are Not Alone." *Wired*. www.wired .com/2009/12/1230hubble-first-galaxy-outside-milky-way/

Hossenfelder, Sabine. "The Superfluid Universe." Aeon Essays. Aeon, 1 February 2016. https://aeon.co/essays/is-dark-matter-subatomic-particles-a-superfluid-or-both?

https://www.aip.org/history-programs/niels-bohr-library/oral-histories/33963

Lightman, Alan P. and Roberta Brawer. Origins: *The Lives and Worlds of Modern Cosmologists*. Cambridge, MA: Harvard University Press, 1990.

Popova, Maria. "Pioneering Astronomer Vera Rubin on Women in Science, Dark Matter, and Our Never-Ending Quest to Know the Universe." *Brain Pickings*, 18 April 2016. www.brainpickings.org/2016/04/18/vera-rubin-interview-women-in-science/

Rubin, Vera C. *Bright Galaxies, Dark Matters*. Woodbury, NY: American Institute of Physics, 1997

Scoles, Sarah. "How Vera Rubin Confirmed Dark Matter." Astronomy. www.astronomy .com/news/2016/10/vera-rubin

MARGARET SANGER: CRUSADER FOR WOMEN'S REPRODUCTIVE FREEDOM

Baker, Jean H. *Margaret Sanger: A Life of Passion*. New York: Hill and Wang, 2011.

"Biographical Sketch." *The Margaret Sanger Papers Project*. www.nyu.edu/projects/sanger

"Connecticut and the Comstock Law." ConnecticutHistory.org. https://connecticuthistory .org/connecticut-and-the-comstock-law/

Eig, Jonathan. *The Birth of the Pill*. New York: W. W. Norton & Co., 2014.

"Margaret Sanger—20th Century Hero." Planned Parenthood. https://www .plannedparenthood.org/files/7513/9611/6635/Margaret_Sanger_Hero_1009.pdf

Margaret Sanger's *The Woman Rebel*—100 Years Old. Margaret Sanger Papers Project, 20 March 2014. https://sangerpapers.wordpress.com/2014/03/20/margaret-sangers-the -woman-rebel-100-years-old/

Sanger, Margaret. "A Public Nuisance." *Birth Control Review*, Oct. 1931. https://www.nyu.edu /projects/sanger/webedition/app/documents/show.php?sangerDoc=225696.xml

———. *Margaret Sanger: An Autobiography*. New York: W. W. Norton & Co., 1938.

Sanger, Margaret. "*Birth Control* (Chicago Address to Women)," Apr–May 1916.

SECOND WAVE FEMINISM: SISTERHOOD BECOMES POWERFUL

Banner, Lois W. *Women in Modern America: A Brief History*. Boston: Cengage Learning, 2004. First published in 1984 by Harcourt Brace Jovanovich.

Baxandall, Rosalyn and Linda Gordon. *Dear Sisters: Dispatches from the Women's Liberation Movement*. New York: Basic Books, 2000.

Boissoneault, Lorraine. "The 1977 Conference on Women's Rights That Split America in Two." 15 February 2017, Smithsonian.com. https://www.smithsonianmag.com/history/1977 -conference-womens-rights-split-america-two-180962174/

Brownmiller, Susan. *In Our Time: Memoir of a Revolution*. New York: Delta, 2000. First published in 1999 by Dial Press.

Cobble, Dorothy Sue, Linda Gordon, and Astrid Henry. *Feminism Unfinished: A Short, Surprising History of American Women's Movements*. New York: Liveright Publishing, 2014.

Collins, Gail. *When Everything Changed: The Amazing Journey of American Women from 1960 to the Present*. New York: Little, Brown and Co., 2009.

Faludi, Susan. *Backlash: The Undeclared War Against American Women*. New York: Crown, 1991.

Friedan, Betty. *The Feminine Mystique*. New York: W. W. Norton & Co., 1963. Fiftieth anniversary edition reissued by W. W. Norton in 2013 with an introduction by Gail Collins and an afterword by Anna Quindlen.

"Highlights." National Organization for Women. now.org/about/history/highlights/

Rosen, Ruth. *The World Split Open: How the Modern Women's Movement Changed America*. New York: Penguin Books, 2006. First published in 2000 by Viking.

Solis, Steph. "Miss America Protest: 6 Things You Probably Didn't Learn in History Class." *USA Today*, 7 September 2016. https://www.usatoday.com/story/news/nation/2016/09/07 /miss-america-protest-1968-things-you-probably-didnt-learn-history-class/89928396/

Sugrue, Anna. "Ms. Gloria Steinem and Second-Wave Feminism." http://steinemsecondwave .weebly.com/

Wolbrecht, Christina. *The Politics of Women's Rights: Parties, Positions, and Change*. Princeton, NJ: Princeton University Press, 2000.

GLADYS TANTAQUIDGEON: CHAMPION OF NATIVE AMERICAN CULTURE

Dunn, Shirley W. *The River Indians: Mohicans Making History*. Fleischmanns, NY: Purple Mountain Press, 2009.

Fawcett, Melissa Jayne, *Medicine Trail: The Life and Lessons of Gladys Tantaquidgeon*. Tucson: University of Arizona Press, 2000.

"Gladys Tantaquidgeon." *Explore*. The Mohegan Tribe. https://www.mohegan.nsn.us/explore /heritage/memoriam/medicine-woman-gladys-tantaquidgeon-memorial

"Gladys Tantaquidgeon, 106, Mohegans' Medicine Woman." *New York Times*, 2 November 2005. https://www.nytimes.com/2005/11/02/us/gladys-tantaquidgeon-106-mohegans-medicine-woman.html

Martin, Douglas. "Tribe's Past and Future Are the Legacy of Its Anthropologist Matriarch at 98." *New York Times*, 4 June 1997. https:// www.nytimes.com/1997/06/04/nyregion/tribe-s-past-and-future-are-the-legacy-of-its-anthropologist-matriarch-at-98.html

"Mohegan-Pequot Diary" (1904) by Fidelia Fielding. dawnlandvoices.org/collections/items/show/282

"Running Against Time: Medicine Woman Preserves Mohegan Culture." *Penn Arts & Sciences*, Summer 2001. www.sas.upenn.edu/sasalum/newsltr/summer2001/running.html

Senier, Siobhan et al., ed. *Dawnland Voices: An Anthology of Indigenous Writing from New England*. Lincoln, NE: University of Nebraska, 2014.

Voight, Virginia Frances. *Mohegan Chief: The Story of Harold Tantaquidgeon*, New York: Funk & Wagnalls, 1965.

IDA MINERVA TARBELL: PIONEER INVESTIGATIVE JOURNALIST

Brady, Kathleen. *Ida Tarbell: Portrait of a Muckraker*. Pittsburgh, PA: University of Pittsburgh Press, 1989.

King, Gilbert. "The Woman Who Took on the Tycoon." https://www.smithsonianmag.com/history/the-woman-who-took-on-the-tycoon-651396

Kochersberger, Robert C., Jr. *More Than a Muckraker: Ida Tarbell's Lifetime in Journalism*. Knoxville: University of Tennessee Press, 2017.

McCully, Emily Arnold. *Ida M. Tarbell: The Woman Who Challenged Big Business—And Won!* Boston: Clarion/Houghton Mifflin Harcourt, 2014.

Piascik, Andy. "Ida Tarbell: The Woman Who Took on Standard Oil." https://connecticuthistory.org/ida-tarbell-the-woman-who-took-on-standard-oil

Roosevelt, Theodore. "The Man with the Muck-rake" (speech delivered 14 April 1906). www.americanrhetoric.com/speeches/teddyrooseveltmuckrake.htm

Tarbell, Ida M. *All in the Day's Work: An Autobiography*. New York: Macmillan, 1939. Reprint, Urbana: University of Illinois Press, 2003.

———. *The Ways of Women*. New York: The Macmillan Company, 1915. Reprint, Forgotten Books, 2017.

Weinberg, Steve. *Taking on the Trust: How Ida Tarbell Brought Down John D. Rockefeller and Standard Oil*. New York: W. W. Norton & Co., 2008.

Yergin, Daniel. *The Prize: The Epic Quest for Oil, Money & Power*. New York: Free Press, 1991.

MADAM C. J. WALKER: MILLIONAIRE BUSINESSWOMAN AND PHILANTHROPIST

Bundles, A'Lelia. *On Her Own Ground: The Life and Times of Madam C.J. Walker*. New York: Scribner, 2001.

Gates, Henry Louis Jr. "Madam Walker, the First Black American Woman to Be a Self-Made Millionaire" in *The African Americans*. PBS. pbs.org/wnet/african-americans-many-rivers-to-cross

Latson, Jennifer. "How America's First Self-Made Female Millionaire Built Her Fortune." http://time.com/3641122/sarah-breedlove-walker/

Lommel, Cookie. *Madam C.J. Walker: Entrepreneur*. Los Angeles: Holloway House, 1993.

Lowry, Beverly. *Her Dream of Dreams: The Rise and Triumph of Madam C.J. Walker*. New York: Vintage Books, 2004.

"Madam C. J. Walker." https://www.history.com/topics/black-history/madame-c-j-walker

Rooks, Noliwe M. *Hair Raising: Beauty, Culture, and African American Women*. New Brunswick, NJ: Rutgers University Press, 1996.

Wintz, Cary D. "The Harlem Renaissance: What Was It, and Why Does It Matter?" *Humanities Texas*, February 2015. http://www.humanitiestexas.org/news/articles/harlem-renaissance-what-was-it-and-why-does-it-matter

ALICE WATERS: CRUSADER FOR SLOW FOOD, AND FOUNDER OF THE EDIBLE SCHOOLYARD

Beard, Alison. "Life's Work: An Interview with Alice Waters." *Harvard Business Review*, 17 Apr. 2017. https://hbr.org/2017/05/alice-waters

Kamp, David. "Cooking Up a Storm." *Vanity Fair*, October 2006. https://www.vanityfair.com/news/2006/10/kamp_excerpt200610

McNamee, Thomas. *Alice Waters and Chez Panisse*. New York: Penguin Press, 2007.

Severson, Kim. "Alice Waters on Sex, Drugs and Sustainable Agriculture." *New York Times*, 22 August 2017. www.nytimes.com/2017/08/22/dining/alice-waters-chef-author-book.html

Waters, Alice. *Coming to My Senses: The Making of a Counterculture Cook*. New York: Clarkson Potter/Publishers, 2017.

———. *Edible Schoolyard: A Universal Idea*. San Francisco: Chronicle Books, 2008.

index